SOCIAL SOLIDARITY
AMONG THE JAPANESE IN SEATTLE

Social Solidarity
among the Japanese in Seattle

S. FRANK MIYAMOTO

With a New Introduction by the Author

UNIVERSITY OF WASHINGTON PRESS, Seattle and London
Published in cooperation with the Asian American Studies Program,
University of Washington

Cover photo (ca. 1914) shows Japanese immigrants standing in front of a dormitory for new arrivals at 915 E. Fir, Seattle, maintained by the Japanese Christian Society. Literally, the sign in the picture reads: "Christian Denominations Kindred Spirit Society." Buddhist as well as Christian groups, and many other associations, were organized to help the new arrivals adjust to the New World. (Photo courtesy of Mrs. Y. Hayashi and Ryo Tsai.)

Social Solidarity among the Japanese in Seattle was originally published in December 1939 in the University of Washington Publications in the Social Sciences, Volume 11, No. 2, pp. 57-130. In 1981 it was reissued as Number 2 in the Occasional Monograph Series of the Asian American Studies Program of the University of Washington. The present edition is published in 1984 by the University of Washington Press in cooperation with the Asian American Studies Program.

Library of Congress Cataloging in Publication Data
Miyamoto, Shotaro Frank, 1912-
    Social solidarity among the Japanese in Seattle.
    "Published in cooperation with the Asian American Studies Program, University of Washington."
    1. Japanese Americans—Washington (State)—Seattle—Social conditions.   2. Seattle (Wash.)—Race relations.
3. Seattle (Wash.)—Social conditions.   I. Title.
F899.S49J35 1984   305.8'956'0797   84-40328
ISBN 0-295-96151-1

FOREWORD TO THE ORIGINAL EDITION, 1939

It will perhaps be of interest to know that in this investigation of the Japanese in Seattle I have studied a people with whom I am thoroughly familiar, having lived in or near their community most of my life. While this familiarity greatly facilitated my research, it is possible, on the other hand, that a bias directed by personal interest and a blindness that comes of too great familiarity entered the analysis of the material. The only guarantee of freedom from such distortions is the degree to which sociological analysis gives objectivity in observing social phenomena.

My greatest indebtedness is to Dr. Jesse J. Steiner who first suggested the problem, and whose thoughtful guidance and constant encouragement were invaluable throughout the investigation. For some of the basic insights into Japanese community life, I owe much to Dr. Forrest LaViolette with whom I had the good fortune to work on related problems. To Dr. Howard B. Woolston, who had less to do with the immediate direction to the study, but whose critical attitude was always held in mind, I wish to express an indebtedness for certain fundamental ways of looking at the problem. Lastly, to the people of the Japanese community, without whose generous aid of time and information this study would have been impossible, I extend my sincere gratitude.

INTRODUCTION TO THE 1981 EDITION

I am very pleased to have my monograph on the Seattle Japanese community reissued under the auspices of the AASP Occasional Monograph Series. The study was done in the mid-1930s as my master's thesis, and it is gratifying that my fledgling research effort still attracts attention over forty years after its first publication.

I have been asked how I came to do this study—an understandable question, for in the 1930s a Nisei who aspired to social research was an uncommon phenomenon, and sociological studies of prewar Japanese communities were also a rarity. Although a high percentage of Nisei of that time period entered college, their choice of college majors strongly emphasized such marketable training as accounting, foreign trade, engineering, pharmacy, law, medicine, and dentistry. Even so the Nisei experienced grave difficulties in finding employment after graduation. Only the foolhardy ventured into such fields as sociology and literature. The truth is, I took two years of engineering and switched to sociology after concluding that for me the pursuit of a subject that genuinely interested me was the less foolhardy course.

Two professors in the Department of Sociology at the University of Washington influenced me critically in my choice of career and research interest. Dr. Jesse F. Steiner, then chairman of the Department, more than any other single individual promoted my career in sociology. He had spent several years teaching in Japan, took a personal interest in Japanese Americans, and was a specialist in community studies. It was no accident that my research attention was drawn to the Japanese community. Just as I was fishing for a thesis subject, Forrest E. LaViolette joined the Washington faculty. He arrived with an interest in research on the Japanese minority and invited me not only to join him in research but also to live in his home. The incomparable schooling in sociology and research which Forrest gave me through this association shaped not only my project but also my lifetime habits of thought about sociology. Sympathetic and sagacious mentors often play a critical role in a student's development, and this is especially true for minority students whose opportunities are restricted.

The community also interested me because I had grown up in it. To be accurate, I grew up both inside and outside the community, and this marginality heightened my interest. Our family moved into a white neighborhood when I was a child, and most of my everyday associates were white children and youths. On the other hand, my father owned a hardware and furniture business in the heart of the Japanese community, and because its success depended on nurturing social as well as commercial relations, our family was regularly involved in the activities of the community. Moreover, the activities and adventures of my cousins, a family of boys who lived in the Japanese community, greatly attracted me, and through them I was drawn into the youth world of the Japanese community. As a child and youth I was only dimly conscious of the contrasts I experienced as I passed from one universe to the other and back again, but I am sure those experiences were a substantial source of my desire to examine the Japanese community more closely and write about it.

What shall I say about my study over four decades after its first publication? It has, I believe, some enduring merits. The chief of them is the fact that it was done and published. Apart from my study there is not, to my knowledge, any other published study of a Japanese minority community before World War II—not of Los Angeles, San Francisco, Sacramento, Gardena, Florin, Hood River, or the dozens of other communities about which we wish we knew more—yet most Japanese minority members on the Pacific Coast before the war lived in or were in some fashion bound to a Japanese community and were significantly influenced by the affiliation. Chie Nakane in her book *Japanese Society* (Berkeley and Los Angeles: Univ. of California Press, 1970) indicates that in Japan the community historically played an unusually powerful and basic role in the lives of its people, more so than in China or India. Not surprisingly, the Japanese immigrants to this country reconstructed the pattern. Hence, the prewar backgrounds of the minority's members generally need to be understood in the context of the communities with which they are associated. My study has the merit, I feel, of preserving something of that picture which otherwise would be almost totally lacking.

The study has the merit also of having focused on the intense organization that was characteristic of those communities. To me this was an obvious and distinct feature, for in contrast to the socially segmented life of most white Americans in the larger community, almost every Japanese minority member seemed in some way linked to an elaborate social network in the Japanese community. Other writers on the Japanese in the United States had noted the characteristic but had not discussed the matter at any length. It may be observed that contemporary sociological writers on Japanese society, especially Nakane cited above, emphasize the elaborate structure of relations that characterizes the society. And recently Ivan Light in *Ethnic Enterprise in America* (Berkeley and Los Angeles: Univ. of California Press, 1972) used the organizational predilection of the Japanese minority, and also of the Chinese minority, as a basis for explaining successful minority adaptation to America. I am now more than ever persuaded that the social relational network of the Japanese community, its social solidarity as I chose to call it, deserved to be studied.

The organization of the Japanese community, however, differed from the structure of impersonal agencies and offices which generally characterizes American communities and rather was based on a network of intimate groups and associations. Sociologists have long recognized a distinction between the intimate versus the impersonal bases of social organization (for example, Maine, Tonnies, Durkheim, Cooley, Redfield, etc.), and in my concluding chapter I refer to the distinction drawn by Ferdinand Tonnies between *Gemeinschaft* (community) and *Gesellschaft* (society) as reflecting the kind of organizational difference I saw between the local Japanese and the white American communities. I must admit that this theoretical discussion could have been omitted without any loss to the study, but I am glad the reference is there, for if the organizational basis of this community is to be explained, I believe account would need to be taken of the kind of distinction I have drawn.

There are many things about this study which I wish I had done differently. First, an M.A. thesis was necessarily a very limited vehicle for serious research, and I now wish I had used it only as a pilot study and mounted a more extensive project on its basis. I am confident the study as published reported the general features of the community accurately enough, but the lack of time and personnel to probe more deeply caused me to miss many refinements of analysis which would have enhanced understanding of the community. In particular, I needed a collaborator or research assistant with reading ability in Japanese. Although I had sufficient command of conversational Japanese to conduct interviews, I had only limited capacity for reading the Japanese newspapers and the numerous records and documents which were available. The community in 1936 was still dominated by the Issei, whose communications were mainly in Japanese, and my inability to read Japanese was a serious handicap.

With more ample means for research, I would have elaborated several lines of analysis, which were only roughly sketched in the published study. In the economic area, I would have investigated in greater detail the various adaptations which were made of the traditional *oyabun-kobun* (parent role–child role) relationship pattern— for example, in the labor contractor system by which workers were recruited for the railroads, sawmills, farms, and salmon canneries, and by which many immigrants got their economic start—and of other traditional organizational means employed by the Japanese minority to make itself economically competitive. I would have discussed the *kenjinkai* (perfectural associations) and their role in organizing relations in the community more fully. And I might have developed a less stereotyped picture of relations in the family. In short, I could have greatly extended and refined the analyses of the community's institutions, associations, and relational networks.

There are two serious gaps in the present study which I would have tried to fill. A notable shortcoming of the study is its failure to present anything like an adequate account of the Nisei society in prewar Seattle. The Nisei were an increasingly significant force in the community, but because the Issei were still dominant, the Nisei society was not well defined and was difficult to describe, and I lacked time to develop this facet of the research, I chose to neglect the Nisei. The other gap lies in my failure to consider the problems of conflict and disorganization which were present in the community, and which the community needed to deal with in order to maintain its social solidarity. The latter in the final analysis was the salient feature, but the lack of reference to stresses gives the misleading impression that I did not observe any problems. To the extent that these gaps are present, my picture of the prewar community is unbalanced.

Despite its deficiencies and its brevity, however, I believe my monograph preserves a picture of the Japanese minority in American before World War II that would be badly missed if it were unavailable. I am therefore happy to have my study reissued in this new form.

INTRODUCTION TO THE 1984 EDITION

It may be asked why I should use the second reprinting of my small monograph as an occasion to write yet another introduction, but I feel something additional is needed. As I noted in my earlier introduction, there are major gaps in my study done almost fifty years ago. To correct the deficiencies would require a full-scale revision and expansion of the piece, and I do intend to carry out such a revision at some future time. In the meantime, however, this reprinting catches me in a mood of dissatisfaction with the study as it is, and of feeling that an effort should be made now to fill some of the gaps.

For this edition I have not attempted any revisions of the text, which is therefore reproduced exactly as it was in the original. Even the bibliography, which could stand a good deal of updating, is left untouched. It has been suggested that I might include here a brief discussion of a number of books bearing significantly on my monograph which have appeared since its original publication. This undertaking I have also decided to save for the full-scale revision. I do, however, want to mention a few works that are particularly pertinent to my study, especially four upon which I have drawn extensively in this introduction: Roger Daniels, *The Decision to Relocate the Japanese Americans* (New York: Lippincott, 1975); Morton Grodzins, *Americans Betrayed* (1949; reprint, Chicago: Univ. of Chicago Press, 1974); Bill Hosokawa, *JACL in Quest of Justice* (New York: Morrow, 1982); and Harry H. L. Kitano, *Japanese Americans* (Englewood Cliffs, N.J.: Prentice Hall, 1969). Two others that deserve special mention are Monica Sone, *Nisei Daughter* (1952; reprint, Seattle and London: Univ. of Washington Press, 1979), a memoir of a prewar Seattle girlhood; and Forrest E. LaViolette, *Americans of Japanese Ancestry* (1945; reprint, 1979), which drew much of its material from the Seattle-area Nisei. Among others that bear significantly on the problems of my study are Edna Bonacich and John Modell, *The Economic Basis of Ethnic Solidarity* (Berkeley and Los Angeles: Univ. of California Press, 1980); Bill Hosokawa, *Nisei* (New York: Morrow, 1969); Peter Irons, *Justice at War* (New York and Oxford: Oxford University Press, 1983); Ivan Light, *Ethnic Enterprise in America* (Berkeley and Los Angeles: Univ. of California Press, 1972); Gene N. Levine and Colbert Rhodes, *The Japanese American Community* (New York: Praeger, 1981); Darrel Montero, *Japanese Americans* (Boulder, Colo.: Westview Press, 1980); John Modell, *The Economics and Politics of Radical Accommodation* (Urbana, Ill.: Univ. of Illinois Press, 1977); and William Peterson, *Japanese Americans, Oppression and Success* (New York: Random House, 1971).

I want to use this introduction to discuss three new topics, two that are expansions of matters briefly touched on in the original, and a third that is totally new. (1) The discussion of the relationship between the Japanese minority and the larger white community before World War II deserves expansion. I gave too little space to this subject in the original with the result that the presentation failed to give a clear sense of the restrictive context within which the minority community existed. (2) The place of the Nisei (the second generation) in the prewar community needs considerable elaboration. In the original study, I minimized attention to this group, partly because my research resources were limited, and partly because I thought a satisfactory account of the community's solidarity could be given by considering the Issei alone. Today, however, it is clear that the picture of the community is unbalanced without a more adequate treatment of the Nisei. (3) I want to add something that could not have been written at the time of the original study, namely, an analysis of how the community's solidarity during the prewar period was related to the wartime evacuation that was to occur in 1942.

I believe all three discussions will enhance the readers' understanding of the prewar Japanese minority community. The first and third topics should give a better sense of the historical context within which the community was moving. And the second topic, on the Nisei, should help to fill an important part of the community's picture that should not have been left as poorly sketched as it was before.

THE STRUCTURE OF MAJORITY-MINORITY RELATIONS

Racial and ethnic minority groups in American society are obviously greatly influenced in their behavior by the majority group's behavior toward them, and a minority group therefore cannot be understood unless its position relative to the majority is clearly delineated. It is not easy, however, to describe briefly the position of the Japanese minority vis-à-vis the majority group in Seattle in the mid-1930s. The general point may be that, before World War II, prejudice and discrimination were much more manifest than they are today, but the degree of prejudice and discrimination needs to be specified more precisely. The simplest way to specify the relationship is to say that it was *castelike*, but that the relationship was not as rigid as the term "caste" implies.

All caste structures bear certain common features. Two of them are often seen wherever prejudice and discrimination occur. (1) The groups are assumed to be culturally and biologically distinguished, and the inferior group is thought to possess notably inferior qualities; and (2) the inferior group is limited to inferior opportunities and rewards. But the next two features are especially distinctive of caste structures. (3) The assumption is that the statuses are hereditary and fixed, and thus members of the inferior group may never rise to the rank of the superior group. (4) The inferior group is excluded from intimate associations with the superior group, that is, inferiors are not allowed to sit in the same area with superiors, eat with them, or bathe with them, and certainly may not marry them. The relationship between the Japanese minority and the majority group was not a rigid caste, for members of the minority occasionally rose quite high in status, sometimes associated closely with the majority, and even married majority group persons. But the relationship was castelike in the sense that the dominant patterns bore many of the features described above.

The Issei, for example, were permanently restricted to an inferior status. Their basic limitation was their ineligibility for citizenship. The Congressional Act of 1790, which decreed that "any alien, being a free white person," is eligible for citizenship, was later modified by Congressional action in 1870 to grant naturalization privileges to "persons of African nativity or descent." These laws were interpreted as not including Orientals. Repeated challenges of the law before the United States Supreme Court by immigrant Japanese, including four cases brought by persons who had served in the United States armed forces, failed to overturn the exclusion. (The Walter-McCarran Act of 1952 subsequently made all races eligible for citizenship.)

Because of their lack of citizenship, all kinds of restrictions were imposed on the Issei. Two legislative restrictions were particularly notable. Alien Land Laws, initially passed in California in 1913, modified in 1920 to plug loopholes, and passed in the state of Washington in 1921, prohibited the sale or lease of land to any alien ineligible for citizenship. These laws severely handicapped Issei farmers and businessmen in addition to impeding their purchase of residential property. In the same period, the passage of the Immigration Act of 1924 specifically excluded aliens ineligible for citizenship from admission as immigrants to the United States. The economic effects of these restrictions were bad enough, but the sense they produced on the Issei of being unwelcome and permanently alien had a profound effect. The Nisei, because they were citizens by birthright, were not directly affected by these laws, but because they necessarily identified with the Issei, they could not avoid the implication of also being unwelcome.

Informal patterns of segregation in the Seattle area were no less important in shaping the climate of a castelike relationship. Occupational segregation was a fundamental limiting condition. Efforts of both Issei and Nisei to gain entry into trade unions were invariably rebuffed, and their acceptance into white companies in other than menial and unskilled capacities was relatively rare. Segregation barriers were also high in many residential areas, and families who tried to find homes outside the polyethnic central area were certain to encounter hostility in some form. Outward residential movement was possible, however, because resistance was low in interstitial areas near shopping centers and heavily trafficked streets, and also because lower-middle-class areas often had no consistent exclusion policy. In other aspects of community life, although no institutionalized "Jim Crow" system existed that explicitly defined areas from which members of the Japanese minority would be excluded, there were many social groups and situations where they were not welcomed. There were uncertainties, for example, about receiving service at restaurants, barbershops, motels, and even some retail shops; there were instances of exclusion from public swimming pools; and there were rumors that minority members would be shunted off to inferior seats in movie theaters. All this reflected a general tendency of the majority group to regard the Japanese minority, both Issei and Nisei, as an essentially alien group whom they preferred to maintain at a considerable social distance.

We want now to consider the effects of this castelike relationship. One effect was to intensify the in-group orientation of the minority and retard their assimilation into American society. Residential and social segregation were at first as much self-imposed as they were externally imposed by majority group restrictions, but the barriers against movement into the white American society unquestionably tended over time to solidify the segregation pattern. Given the difficulty of surmounting the segregation barriers, the minority learned to live within its own group, create conditions within the community which would make life interesting and enjoyable and compensate for the shortcomings of a less attractive residential district, and protect the group from the pain of repeated rejections by the majority group. The establishment of *Nihon-machi* ("Japan Town"), with its small but active business center, its cluster of Japanese minority residences in the surrounding area, and its collection of institutions and organizations, aroused little objection from the majority group. The Japanese community therefore flourished, but this segregation pattern had the harmful effect of reinforcing the majority group's prejudices against the minority, and minimizing the latter's opportunities for learning how to win acceptance in the larger society.

The most profound effect of the segregation pattern was on the attitudes of the majority and the minority groups toward each other. On the whole, the majority group viewed the Issei immigrants as aliens who lacked socially desirable qualities and were unassimilable. The Nisei, to be sure, were regarded as quite Americanized, but because they were still relatively young had relatively little influence on the perception of the minority as a whole.

The Issei initially accepted their alien status, for on the whole their intention at first was to return to Japan after accumulating savings. As their families grew, however, and their futures became increasingly committed to this country, their outcast status was more and more an aggravation to them, although they generally resigned themselves to the limitation. Their energy was directed toward advancing themselves economically and toward the variety of activities that were generated within the ethnic community. And their hopes were pinned on the Nisei, on the belief that, though they themselves were restricted, the Nisei with their advantages would be able to overcome the segregation barriers.

As for the Nisei, the ambiguities in their attitudes reflected the ambiguities in the environment in which they grew up. They were trained in the textbooks and activities of the American public schools. They learned to pledge allegiance to the American flag, to sing the national anthem, and to take pride in the glories of the American past. They were attracted to the same movies, the same popular songs, the same dance steps, and the same sports as the rest of American youths. So they saw themselves as Americans and aspired to the same goals as other American youths. And they were aware of the continuing national emphasis on the Americanization of immigrant groups. As sociologist Milton Gordon has pointed out, however, Americanization in that period was understood to mean "Anglo conformity," conformance with the ways of behavior of the white Anglo-Saxon Protestant group. The paradox for the Nisei was that as they tried to conform to Anglo ways, they repeatedly ran into barriers that obstructed their access to the Anglo way of life. It is of interest that in the mid-1930s the Nisei spent a good deal of time in self-examination and in discussions of their assimilation problems. In another ten years they would have seen much more clearly that the problems were not within themselves but in the castelike social structure that excluded them from significant opportunities in American life.

The Nisei of Prewar Seattle

The Nisei, the children of the immigrants, were an element in the community almost from its beginning, but because they were at first young and less numerous, they played before 1930 a secondary role in the community. By 1936, however, they were an emerging community force, and by 1942, following the outbreak of World War II, the Nisei suddenly displaced the Issei in power. The shifting relationship between the two generations is reflected in the changing demography of the two groups over decennial periods: 378 Nisei (6 percent) of 6,127 total in 1910; 1,863 Nisei (24 percent) in 1920; 4,000 (47 percent) in 1930; and 4,268 (61 percent) in 1940. By 1940, the median ages of the Issei and Nisei, respectively, were about fifty and eighteen years. The sharp break in age between the two generations was caused by the Immigration Act of 1924, which in that year stopped all further immigration of the Issei.

The story of the Nisei in the early years was necessarily closely tied to the careers of the developing immigrant families: how the parents made a living, where they lived, and what activities interested the families. By 1910, *Nihon-machi*, the busy trade district of the Japanese minority community, was clearly centered on Sixth Avenue and Main Street, at the southern edge of the central business district, in the shadow of the forty-two-story L. C. Smith Building (acclaimed the tallest building in the West) and a figurative stone's throw from the railroad station. Because the Issei very early established themselves in various city trades, numerous Issei shops and offices clustered around the center, and immigrant family residences surrounded this center. Intermixed with the Japanese businesses and residences, but almost wholly separated from them interactionally, were saloons, gambling joints, and houses of prostitution. Impressionistically, an outsider might have seen this district as the slum area of Seattle, but the external appearance belied the highly organized life maintained by the Japanese community and families.

Some Nisei had their first homes in the hotels and apartment houses which their parents operated in the Skid Road or International District areas, or in back rooms behind grocery stores, barber shops, laundries, and other shops established by the Issei parents. Many more grew up in an area east of *Nihon-machi*, an elevated section called First Hill, where many single-family and multiple-family units, typically aging clapboard structures, were to be found. The majority of these houses were occupied by Japanese families. Because the two principal streets, Washington and Main, of this area were unpaved and traffic was consequently light, Nisei children and youths often took them over for their playgrounds. Lifelong friendships were established in street groups formed in this area. Other family residences were scattered farther out in areas contiguous to the central core. Finally, a distinct residential pattern should be mentioned, the tendency of some Japanese families to move a considerable distance away from the center. These outward moves often occurred in conjunction with the location of a business (grocery, cleaner, nursery, and so on) or farm in an outlying area. Nisei growing up in these homes often had less early association with other Nisei, but they were rarely totally disconnected from the Japanese community.

Life in these homes was a mix of the Japanese and the American. The furniture and appliances were invariably American, but the fabrics, the dishware, the artwork, the family shrine (especially in Buddhist homes), and many other features often gave a distinctly Japanese air to the home. Reading materials were both English and Japanese, and food was generally an alternate mix of the two. Birthday parties were observed in the western mode, but the dolls festival (*hina-matsuri*), the display of formal Japanese dolls for girl children, was necessarily a Japanese affair. The most western events in the home were probably Thanksgiving and Christmas, while the most Japanese was New Year's Day. For this, the Issei housewife invariably spent days in housecleaning and food preparation with the children's help. New Year's was a day for rounds of house visits by the men, with much feasting and drinking, and children were carefully taught the ritual New Year's greeting so that they might properly meet the guests.

The immigrant family seldom existed as an entity separate from a social network of relatives, *kenjin* (prefectural countrymen), employer and employees, and friends, and through these contacts the Nisei spontaneously learned a great deal about Japanese conceptions of social relationships. A *kenjin*—a person from one's own perfecture such as Hiroshima, Yamaguchi, and Fukuoka—was someone with whom the Issei felt a natural closeness because he came from the same province, and to whom he was in some degree duty-bound. In all these relationships two traditional Japanese conceptions were clearly evident: the Japanese tendency to favor group action in dealing with any critical event, and the rules of obligations that bind people together in the networks mentioned above. More will be said about this later. Nisei could not fail to observe and learn that births, marriages, deaths, or any other critical family events were occasions for group action—in fact, that a virtual formal mechanism for group action pre-existed—and that, for various circumstances, complex rules of obligation bound people together.

In all immigrant communities the immigrant and offspring generations (parents and children) experience problems of relationships between them owing to differences of cultural background. For several reasons, these problems in the Japanese immigrant community (and probably for the Chinese as well) were especially acute: (1) the Japanese and American cultures differed greatly; (2) both parents and children generally were limited in their ability to speak the other's language; (3) the widespread anti-Japanese agitation of the majority group emphasized to the Nisei the disadvantages of adhering to the Japanese culture; and (4) the Issei interpreted the same antagonism as reason to question the Nisei's trust of the American people. Despite these differences, however, the parents were able to maintain an exceptional degree of control over their children—for example, the Nisei had by far the lowest delinquency rate of any group in the city—and we should try to understand how those controls were effected.

An essential element in the Issei's child-training practices was the amount of attention the parents, especially the mother, gave to the children. Mothers spent a great amount of time attending to their children's needs, and even if a mother worked in a family business or farm, she typically found ways of maintaining contact and supervision over the children. Related to this was their training of children in obligatory relations, the principle that an act of thoughtfulness, kindness, or giving by another must not go unacknowledged or unreciprocated. The training ranged from frequent reminders of courtesies as well as gift-giving relations which needed to be observed, to instruction on such difficult Japanese concepts as *on*, reciprocity relations that bind superiors and inferiors. The reciprocal obligations binding parents and children were, of course, emphasized. Finally, we should at least mention, in this brief account of child training, that the concern for status that is so central to the Japanese system was also transmitted to the Nisei. Perhaps the most basic lesson concerned the importance of maintaining family status (the family name), that a person should not allow his name and therefore the family name to be tarnished. There were lessons also about the importance of status achievement, of avoiding shame, and of obedience to authority, all related to status concerns.

Underlying the patterns of obligations characteristic of the Japanese is a distinctive style of interpersonal interaction which the Nisei also learned. This style of interaction deserves careful elucidation, for the Nisei personality is most readily understood as a product of an adaptation between the Japanese and the markedly different American interpersonal styles. All human interaction involves a process of acting and reacting between self and others, in which the person perceives the behavior of another and adjusts his own responses accordingly. Self-evaluations, the process of looking back upon the self and judging the merits of one's own behavior, are also involved. The Japanese style of interaction requires a high degree of sensitivity to the other, of judging how the other feels about a situation and what motivates the other's behavior; and it also requires high awareness of the self, of how one's own behavior appears to others and will be interpreted by others.

One effect of such interpersonal sensitivity is a reduction in the spontaneity of responses. Spontaneity means more or less reflexive actions in response to one's own feelings, but spontaneity is in direct contradiction to the Japanese interactional style, which requires taking careful account of each other's feelings before acting. American interaction patterns, on the other hand, are less constrained by interpersonal sensitivity requirements and much more spontaneous. This is not to say that Japanese totally lack spontaneity or that Americans are totally without interpersonal sensitivity—both characteristics are obviously abundantly present in both cultures—but there is a greater requirement of interpersonal sensitivity among Japanese than among Americans and a corresponding reduction of spontaneity. The formalism of the Japanese—the time taken, for example, in an everyday greeting with deep bows and ritual exchanges of proprieties—may be seen as a device for aiding the "account taking" of each other's feelings by slowing the pace and by reducing the spontaneity requirements of the interaction.

The Nisei, trained in the Japanese interactional style but exposed to numerous relations with Americans, had personalities which were a mix of these backgrounds. Inevitably, they had the sensitivities typical of the Japanese, though perhaps not as acutely as the Japanese. Spontaneity was not and is not characteristic of the Nisei, but, on the other hand, they found it awkward to adopt the formalism of the Japanese because of its inappropriateness in American relations. In place of formalism, which I consider a ritual means of the Japanese to shield sensitivities, the Nisei employ other devices for shielding themselves. For example, especially among the males, joking relations, which are a way of interacting with the implication that none of this is serious, are extensively used. Nisei often use a Japanese ploy of making indirect rather than direct references, or of being noncommittal where other Americans would tend to be committal. And Nisei conversations often sound "chopped up" because of the shortness of their remarks, which I interpret as a tendency of the speakers to stop for feedback before proceeding.

Given this background, it may be understandable why the Nisei often appear reserved and deliberate compared to other Americans. On the whole, Nisei reflect low rates of impulsivity in their behavior. The Nisei's *enryo* syndrome, about which Dr. Harry Kitano has written, may also be understood. *Enryo* refers to the disposition to restrain one's own action, that is, to sublimate one's own motive or interest in order to accommodate the interest of another. The term is commonly used, for example, when a hostess encourages a guest to eat without *enryo*, implying that there is ample food for everyone, but may also be applied when a person is unassertive where he might be expected to be assertive. *Enryo* typically occurs where persons tend to have a high degree of sensitivity to others, where the concern for others overshadows the concern for self-interest. Pathological cases of *enryo* occur where a person lacks what the Freudian calls "ego strength," an ability to define one's own position in contrast to that of others and a capacity to defend it. The Nisei are not generally pathologically disposed to *enryo*, but they are not a notably assertive group. On the other hand, although it has been claimed that the Nisei are often regarded favorably by others because of their unassertiveness, I suspect rather that their attractiveness, to the extent it exists, lies more in their interpersonal sensitivity.

The Nisei acquired these traits of the Japanese relational system not because their parents repeatedly preached about them but because the Nisei, in their day-to-day life, found themselves frequently involved in associations with Issei relatives, *kenjin*, and family friends. One might call this participatory learning. Returning now to the question posed earlier, as to how the Issei were able to control their children's behavior despite the numerous cultural conflicts, I believe the answer lies in the sense of interdependency and personal responsibility which Nisei acquired through the kinds of interactions described above.

Because of the Issei's slow rate of assimilation into American society, the family was largely a source of Japanese training for the Nisei. The public school, by contrast, was their chief source of Americanization. The kind of Americanization which they received, however, was conditioned by the fact that the elementary schools which the Nisei attended were often heavily enrolled with Nisei and were almost like Japanese community schools.

The first such school, the Main Street School, was located at the heart of the Japanese business district. Its principal, Miss Ada Mahon, a strict no-nonsense kind of teacher who emphasized the traditional values in school instruction, was considered by the Japanese community a most admirable head. At this school as well as at Bailey Gatzert, a new larger structure which she took over in the mid-1920s, she and her staff of white middle-class women teachers taught the Nisei about America by daily performances of the pledge of allegiance, the national anthem, and by instruction concerning American heroes and events. Many Nisei attended other schools as well, but their experiences were on the whole not greatly different. Nisei in those years knew a great deal about George Washington and Abraham Lincoln, but often knew little about comparable Japanese figures such as Toyotomi Hideyoshi and Tokugawa Iyeyasu. The notable point is that the Nisei, socially isolated as they were from the American people, received an idealized picture of American society, modified by ideas received from the movies, newspapers, and magazines. As they advanced into high school and college and participated more extensively in the larger society, they naturally gained a more realistic understanding of America, but their education about

America initially was often restricted and distorted.

Young people, however, probably learned as much from their peers as from their teachers, and here their Americanization was quite direct. When the Nisei entered high schools, they were exposed to large student bodies of white students with whom they developed some degree of association. Whatever the level of association, they were inevitably influenced by the prevalent American student culture: its emphases on sports, movies, popular songs, clothing styles, mannerisms, the latest dance steps, and dating.

Most Nisei also attended a Japanese-language school, usually held for about ninety minutes each day after the regular school ended. It might be thought that the language school would have exerted a Japanizing effect on the Nisei, and in a limited sense it did. The school taught not only language, but also Japanese concepts of status relations (teacher and student), courtesies, the Japanese moral code, and Japanese custom. On special occasions, such as *Tencho-setsu* ("Emperor's Day"), school assemblies with parents present were held at the main community hall, the well-known Nippon Kan hall, and prominent Issei leaders would orate on the significance of the occasion. From such events, the Nisei learned about Japanese attitudes and values, and about Japanese behavior. On the other hand, because of the difficulties of the Japanese language, particularly of learning to read the characters, very few Nisei gained much from the formal schooling, and most regarded it as an onerous duty accepted only to satisfy parental demand. But the school fulfilled an unintended serendipitous function. Like the regular public schools, and also the community's ethnic churches, which will be described below, the language school offered a regular occasion for Nisei to socialize with each other. The school thus extended and intensified the Nisei's involvement in the Nisei social network, and contributed a lasting basis of Nisei solidarity.

The churches were a major institutional function in the local community. All the major Christian denominations (Baptist, Congregational, Episcopalian, Methodist, Presbyterian, and Catholic) had their separate ethnic churches, with strong enrollments of Issei parents and Nisei children. The Buddhist churches, particularly the Jodo Shinshu and Nichiren churches, the two main denominations, were equally well enrolled. These churches unquestionably fulfilled a spiritual role for the memberships, but the spiritual effects are difficult to assess. Their social functions, on the other hand, were clear and significant, especially so for the Nisei.

Most Issei came from Japan with a Buddhist background, and in this country a Buddhist church was for many a natural choice; but perhaps because church affiliations had seldom been strong in Japan, and Christian affiliations were functionally appealing in the United States, surprising numbers of Issei joined Christian churches after immigrating to Seattle. Whichever church the immigrant joined, he was often initially attracted to the church because relatives, *kenjin*, or other friends encouraged his attendance, and perhaps because church memberships tended to be correlated with relational networks, the memberships were notably stable. The Nisei children of immigrant families, therefore, were also likely to share long careers of attending the same church kindergarten, Sunday School classes, and young people's organizations.

Churches of the 1920s and 1930s, it will be remembered, had fewer competing Sunday activities to contend with than churches today, but the Issei had additional reasons for regular church attendance. As immigrants in America, the Issei missed the closeness of personal ties which the family, village, and neighborhood systems of Japan so strongly emphasized, and they found in the church a means of gratifying a need that otherwise was not easily met. The regular Sunday meetings provided weekly occasions for reaffirming interpersonal ties, the ceremonialism and frequent holiday celebrations characteristic of the churches were a common feature of Japanese society and therefore readily appreciated by the Issei, and the activities promoted by the churches fitted easily into the organizational proclivity of the Issei. The Nisei as children went along with their parents' interest and in due course became caught up in their own reasons for a very active church involvement.

The young people's organizations of the churches—the Christian Endeavors and Epworth Leagues of the Christian churches and the Lotus Seinenkai of the Buddhist Church—illustrate the social functions which the ethnic churches performed for the Nisei. Many Nisei gained their first experience with organizational roles and leadership in these clubs. Their socials, which the Nisei generally organized totally independent of Issei supervision since the latter had little concept of how such events were fashioned in America, were often settings for the Nisei's first experience with boy-girl relations. Musical and dramatic events were a means of giving expression to Nisei talent. And the church bazaars, which all the Japanese churches discovered were extraordinarily popular events in spite of the frequency with which they were held, were for the Nisei a chance to show their entrepreneurial skills.

The major annual event for the Christian young people was the Young People's Christian Conference, organized interdenominationally among all the Christian churches in Washington and Oregon. Each year as many as two hundred young people, representing all denominations, would assemble for a two-day conference in Seattle, Portland, Tacoma, Yakima, or wherever a large enough community of Japanese existed to sponsor such an event. Groups organized auto transport to the site of the conference, the local churches mobilized housing and meals for the visiting delegates, and the young people organized the program of speakers and discussions. From our viewpoint, the notable feature of these gatherings was their function in extending the Nisei's social network.

A similar organization with similar functions existed among the Buddhist youths. The Young Buddhist Association, in fact, was a national organization whose annual conference generally brought together representatives from all the Pacific Coast communities.

Socially, then, the ethnic church performed two important functions for the Nisei. First, it established interpersonal ties of unusually enduring quality and also laid relational networks which spanned regional communities. Second, it fulfilled social functions for the Nisei which for white youths were often fulfilled by high school or other organizational activities.

Athletic teams, particularly in basketball, were another activity promoted by many of the churches, but sports in Nisei society had a much broader significance than as a church function, and the subject requires a separate discussion. Nisei boys were always much attracted to the major American sports—baseball, football, and basketball—and in the heyday of the Japanese community, in the 1920s and 1930s, it was commonplace to see boys of all ages involved in pickup games at several street corners on Washington and Main streets and on vacant lots of the district. As youngsters, many proved highly skilled in the sports, but by their late teens the Nisei's lack of physical size was a serious handicap, and very few were good enough to win high school letters. It was thus a reflection of the Nisei's competitiveness and the Issei's high aspirations for Nisei success in competition that in the early 1920s the Nisei fielded two teams, named Asahi and Mikado (later Nippon A.C. and Taiyo A.C.), which played all the sports with moderate success in the City League against white teams.

As the number of Nisei youth increased, however, the community's sports interest shifted to competition among Nisei teams rather than with outsiders. Dozens of Nisei sports clubs mushroomed, organized at different age levels. Long before the Little Leagues and Babe Ruth Leagues were established in the larger community, Nisei teams with distinct names and uniforms were organized into leagues for different age levels to play at whatever sport was in season. The teams were not restricted to Seattle; several came from farming communities in the surrounding area, and from as far away as Tacoma. Girls' teams were also organized, but in those years gained only limited popularity. On the other hand, girls as well as Issei parents were a highly vocal part of the sports scene as loyal supporters of one or another team. Considering the amount of time and effort that went into organizing and financing the many sports clubs, mobilizing and training the players, and maintaining them in leagues at different levels, it must be evident that sports exerted a strong organizing influence on Nisei society.

In addition to the team sports, a golfers' association, a tennis club, a fishermen's club, a judo club, a *kendo* (fencing) club, and a bowling league reflected the wide range of sports interests to be found in this community; and the ubiquitous disposition toward organizing any activity that attracted more than a handful of people could also be seen.

The flourishing of the sports leagues in the Seattle Japanese community owed much to James Y. Sakamoto (b. 1903) and his English-language weekly, the *Japanese American Courier*. Sakamoto was a gifted athlete who in the early 1920s went East to attend college, but ended up in professional boxing in New York City fighting matches at the Madison Square Garden. In 1927, when he found himself going blind, he returned to Seattle and, with financial assistance from his father's meager savings, the steadfast support of his wife Misao, and the aid of talented news-writing friends, he started publication of the *Courier* on 1 January 1928 and continued it until the evacuation in 1942. Because of his interest in sports, sports events were always well covered in his paper. It was the *Courier* that conceived the idea of organizing all the independent Nisei teams in the community, and the resulting organization came to be known as the Courier League.

But it was not only in sports that the *Courier* exerted an organizing influence. In addition to sports and church activities, the paper reported on the many varied activities of the Seattle-area Nisei. Two of the most prominent were the Japanese Students Club and Fuyo-kai, the Nisei men's and women's organizations, respectively, on the University of Washington campus. Because Nisei were excluded from the Greek fraternities and sororities, a men's residence was purchased with community help (the women had no house) in which the usual functions of a fraternity were carried on. Because the Nisei students on campus had extensive ties with the local community, these organizations were more heavily involved in community affairs than student organizations normally are. For the noncollege women, there were the Girls' Club and the Business Girls' Club, which sponsored such activities as dances and socials, oratorical contests, and flower arrangement exhibits. There were music groups such as the Toyo Music Club, the Aeolian Choir, and the Broadway High Jazz Band. There were a Japanese dance school and dance groups, a ham radio club, and a camera club. And there were clubs in the outlying areas, such as Green Lake and Bellevue, which often exchanged functions with central community organizations. The proliferation of Nisei clubs was due to organizing motives inherent in Nisei society itself, but the *Japanese American Courier* clearly served a stimulating and facilitating function by the publicity and encouragement it gave to the organizations.

The most important Nisei organization in the community was the Japanese Americans Citizens League, which James Sakamoto and his newspaper were instrumental in establishing. As early as 1921, when the Anti-Alien Land Law was being legislated in the state of Washington, a small group of Nisei, with the encouragement of Issei who were concerned about the law, formed the Seattle Progressive Citizens League for the purpose of combating discrimination against the Japanese minority. Over the years, the organization barely continued its existence. In 1927, when Sakamoto returned to Seattle, he found the Nisei community split by a bitter conflict between the two clubs, the previously mentioned Nippon A.C. and Taiyo A.C., and he saw the Progressive Citizens League as a device for bringing the warring factions together. Moreover, from the first issue of the *Courier*, Sakamoto used his paper to promote the League. At that time, Nisei groups in California were trying to establish similar organizations. At a meeting of Nisei leaders convened in San Francisco in 1929, it was agreed that a national organization of the Nisei called the National Council of the Japanese American Citizens League should be established, and because Sakamoto and the two friends whom he sent as Seattle representatives were the most active leaders in its promotion, Seattle was chosen as the site of the first national convention of the Japanese American Citizens League, held in 1930.

The League today is by all odds the most important Nisei organization, both locally and nationally, but in the decade of the thirties it struggled to maintain itself. Its various social functions—the annual banquet, the occasional socials and dances, and its "Japan Day" at a recreation park—attracted attention. But the ostensible basic purposes for which it was founded, to raise the Nisei's political consciousness and to fight discrimination, were barely maintained as recognizable aims through Sakamoto's constant editorializing in his paper and by the persistent leadership of a small group of friends.

During the 1930 decade there were several difficulties about the Japanese American Citizens League and its aims. First, the Issei continued to dominate the community, organizationally and economically, and except for a few older Nisei like Sakamoto, very few had experiences which could serve as the basis of strong political convictions. Second, the Nisei were slow in gaining political maturity. Not only were they young, but their political training was minimal. Because the Issei lacked citizenship, or even the eligibility for naturalization, they took little interest in American politics. Moreover, when political discussions might have occurred between parents and children, the language barrier was a serious obstacle to such discussions. Third, the leadership of the organization, both locally and nationally, lacked experience and skill, and their finances were much too limited to support the kinds of programs needed. The lack of national leadership reflected itself in a tendency toward an aimless functioning of the local chapters.

In conclusion, what can be said concerning the Nisei's contribution to the social solidarity of the Japanese community in Seattle? The obvious fact is that the Nisei developed the same disposition toward organizing that was exhibited by the Issei. Indeed, Nisei youths could scarcely remain uninvolved in the organized functions of the Seattle Japanese community. But there were two other basic processes contributing to the solidarity of the community. One was the Nisei's assimilation of the Japanese interpersonal style, modified to fit the American scene, and the resulting emergence of a Nisei culture and associative patterns with which the Nisei felt themselves especially comfortable. The Japanese value system applying to social relationships, particularly the idea of obligatory relations, which in the case of the Issei was a fundamental basis of their solidarity, was also in subtle ways assimilated by the Nisei. The other basic process that deserves notice is the development among the Nisei of interpersonal networks which in later years have proved extremely enduring.

RELATIONSHIP OF SOCIAL SOLIDARITY TO THE EVACUATION

We now know that this community, which in 1938 at the time of my study was so innocently engrossed in carrying on its everyday activities, would less than four years later be destroyed by a fearful catastrophe: a total uprooting of the community by a forced evacuation of the population. The question arises, could these people, had they the omniscience we now possess, have done anything to prevent the impending disaster? But the attempt to answer such a question, I fear, is likely to prove speculative and sterile. I believe we can more profitably ask a different question: in light of what we know today, how was the nature of the community as I have described it related to the evacuation decision that would be reached four years later? The attempt to answer the latter question should add to our understanding of both the community and the evacuation.

The cause of the Japanese minority's evacuation is a subject that requires a book for its proper analysis, but I shall try to sketch the essentials in a few paragraphs. The evacuation was put into effect by the acts of two men. On 19 February 1942, less than two and one-half months after Pearl Harbor, President Franklin D. Roosevelt issued his Executive Order 9066 authorizing any designated military commander to prescribe military areas from which any or all persons might be excluded. Two weeks later, on 3 March 1942, General John L. DeWitt, military commander of the Western Defense Command, issued Public Proclamation No. 1, which designated the western third of the Pacific coast states as a military area from which all persons of Japanese ancestry were excluded. In a matter of weeks thereafter, the forced removal of the Japanese minority was under way. The evacuation, however, was not the independent decision of just these two men, so we need to ask who influenced their decisions.

From the first day of the war, Attorney General Francis Biddle and his assistants were unwavering opponents of the evacuation, especially of the citizens of Japanese ancestry, and they were the chief defenders in the federal government of Japanese American interests. Biddle was certain that the FBI, a division within his department, had from years of scrutinizing the Japanese communities ample knowledge of the security risks posed by the population, and he accepted the agency's assurance that the population could be controlled without an evacuation. His office maintained its position until the final capitulation around 17 February 1942. On the other hand, General DeWitt vacillated back and forth on the question. He obviously was keenly conscious of the charges of negligence brought against General Walter C. Short and Admiral Husband E. Kimmel, the commanding officers at Pearl Harbor at the time of the Japanese attack, and DeWitt was hypersensitive to the continued presence in the coastal areas of people whom he regarded as potential saboteurs. There were investigative reports from highly regarded officers stating that a Japanese military invasion of the Pacific Coast was quite unlikely, and also military intelligence reports assuring that the Japanese minority was not a serious security risk. But DeWitt was also receiving conflicting advice on the other side. Overall, one gets the impression that DeWitt would not have ordered the evacuation had he not been swayed by other influences.

Two men in the War Department in Washington, D.C.—Major General Allen W. Gullion, provost marshal general for the army and as such its chief law enforcement officer, and Colonel Karl R. Bendetsen, chief of his Aliens Division—exerted a crucial influence on General DeWitt. Very early in the war both Generals DeWitt and Gullion became gravely concerned that the Department of Justice was not doing enough about enemy alien control on the Pacific Coast, and in the last week of December 1941, therefore, General Gullion sent Bendetsen to General DeWitt's office in San Francisco to assist in tightening the control program. Through the concerted efforts of DeWitt, Gullion, and Bendetsen, pressure was brought on the Department of Justice to adopt stricter regulations of enemy alien control. As the month of January 1942 advanced, Bendetsen, in whom General DeWitt came to have a good deal of confidence, appears to have advised the latter to use increasingly stringent restrictive measures over the Japanese minority, both citizens and aliens. And as a communication link between DeWitt and Gullion and also with other influential officials of the War Department, Bendetsen appears to have played a critical role in shaping the department's policy on the evacuation question.

The sentiment in support of evacuation was mobilized in less than a month beginning about 16 January 1942. Scattered talk of the need to remove the West Coast Japanese minority was heard from the first days of war, and there is no doubt that pressure groups became active quite early in promoting the evacuation idea. Beginning in January 1942, the mass media played a particularly significant role in promoting the evacuation concept. On 4 January 1942, Damon Runyon, a well-known syndicated columnist, wrote a column in the California papers that warned of the dangers of the Japanese American presence. And starting on 5 January, John B. Hughes, a Los Angeles radio news commentator for the Mutual Broadcasting Company, continued daily for more than a month speaking at length on the dangers of Japanese American sabotage. Hughes may have been the single most important provocateur for evacuation. From mid-January on, the news media of the Pacific Coast followed a trend parallel to that of the region's Congressional leaders in their rising crescendo of voices calling for the evacuation of the Japanese minority.

Probably the first Congressman to speak openly about evacuating the Japanese minority was Congressman Leland Ford of Los Angeles, who by mid-January was dispatching letters to Cabinet-level officers, and on 20 January was the first to speak on the floor of the House about the need for evacuation. About the same time, California Congressmen Clarence Lea, Alfred J. Elliott, and John Z. Anderson were also talking of the need to evacuate the Japanese minority and were prime movers in assembling a caucus of West Coast representatives on 29 and 30 January. By the latter dates a majority of the West Coast Congressmen and Senators, with a few notable exceptions, were actively and effectively campaigning for the removal of the Japanese minority from the Pacific Coast states. On the West Coast, the local politicians, who were a little late in joining the campaign, added their voices by the end of January.

With the pressure groups, the mass media, and local politicians of the Pacific Coast states mobilized to give a clear impression of a concerted public demand for evacuation, and the Congressional delegation in Washington organized to direct the demand to the most critical executive officers, the final act of this decision-making drama was played out in the first two weeks of February 1942 between a handful of people in the War Department and the Justice Department. It appears that General Gullion and Colonel Bendetsen were the two chief proponents of evacuation in the War Department, and in the first week of February they convinced General DeWitt and Assistant Secretary of War John J. McCloy of the need for evacuation. McCloy then won the support of Secretary of War Henry L. Stimson, and Stimson in turn gained President Roosevelt's agreement. In the meantime Attorney General Biddle and his staff were neutralized by the line-up of power on the other side.

Despite the necessary lack of detail in this brief account, it may suffice to give the sense that the following factors conditioned the evacuation decision. First, all the men most directly involved in the decision had almost no knowledge of the Japanese minority, the people whose fate they were judging. In fact, it is striking that those who did have firsthand knowledge of the Japanese minority—the FBI and the military intelligence officers—all attested to their low security risk; but in the decision process, little credence was given to these intelligence reports. Second, the foregoing should suggest that prejudice against the Japanese minority played a crucial part in shaping the decision. For one thing, the pressure groups, the news media, the popular sentiment, and the political leaders of the Pacific Coast all clearly reflected the region's traditional prejudice against the minority. Further, for the decision makers the facts contained in the intelligence reports had far less significance than the prejudiced opinions conveyed to them from a multitude of sources. It may be noted that Attorney General Biddle was not more knowledgeable about the Japanese minority than the others, but he opposed the evacuation on legal grounds, the unconstitutionality of evacuating citizens without due process, and because of his greater faith in the FBI, one of his own agencies. Third, the issue was considered in a climate wholly unfavorable to the Japanese minority: the Japanese were charged with treachery at Pearl Harbor, and by implication Japanese Americans might be regarded as potentially treacherous; American forces were faring badly in the Pacific War, heavy casualties were being suffered, and the desire for vengeance was widespread; and the federal government urgently needed to get the evacuation question out of the way so that attention could be concentrated on carrying on the war. Fourth, the final decision was made by a small group of men, leading one to ask what difference of outcome might have occurred if two or three others had shared Francis Biddle's skepticism toward the evacuation.

We return to the question that was posed at the beginning of this section: was there any relationship between the characteristics of the community in 1938 and the evacuation decision four years later? The evidence indicates that the wartime demand for the removal of the Japanese minority population from Pacific Coast areas arose because Japan's attack on Pearl Harbor and her initial successes in the Pacific war triggered emotions that were deeply embedded in the majority group's historical prejudice against the minority. That is, we regard the historical prejudice as the chief predisposing condition on which events played to produce the evacuation decision. But we now want to trace the earlier career of this prejudice, to show that the same regional prejudice was responsible for producing the kind of segregated community we have described, and to show further that the majority group's perceptions of the segregated community tended to reinforce their original prejudice.

The regional prejudice against the Japanese minority had the character of what sociologist Robert Merton calls a "self-fulfilling prophecy." Prejudice bred segregation; segregation bred an internal system of behavior within the minority that was poorly understood by the majority; and the misperceptions of the minority bred increased prejudice—that is, the minority's behavior reactions to the initial prejudice was seen by the majority group as evidence justifying the initial prejudice. This is the connection I see between the community of 1938 and the evacuation decision four years later. Of course, what was true of the Seattle Japanese minority community alone would not have brought about an action against the whole minority population of the Pacific Coast, but I assume that all the Japanese minority communities of the region were affected in basically similar ways by the regional prejudice.

The fact that the historical prejudice influenced the shape of the community has already been touched on and requires only a brief summary. Exclusion from numerous lines of occupational opportunity and the resulting economic segregation were important factors in the build-up of an ethnic economy; residential segregation induced the clustering of the minority population; and social segregation influenced the development of the community's organizational complex. Interaction among these segregation patterns produced the close-knit community we have described. To be sure, segregation was not totally due to external imposition; it was in part self-imposed. But there were serious limitations in the segregated community, and if attractive outside opportunities had been accessible, it seems highly likely that many would have sought their fortunes outside.

Discriminatory policies such as the exclusion of the Issei from citizenship had the greatest effect on the "self-fulfilling" process. Because of the exclusion, the Issei's involvement in those activities which would have accelerated their assimilation—such as American politics, particularly local politics, which often affected their lives—was diminished. By the same token, their Japanese orientation persisted, and the activities promoted by the Issei tended to have a noticeably Japanese aura about them. Similarly, residential segregation had the effect of promoting interactions among the Japanese residents and of encouraging the development of a parochial subculture. The evidence is clear that Japanese minority communities that were subjected to the heaviest segregationist pressures were generally much less assimilated into American society than those that were least segregated.

In 1942 the charges directed against the Japanese minority which served as reasons for their evacuation included such widely held claims as: it is impossible to comprehend the Japanese mind, any Japanese child who has attended the language schools is a potential enemy, they have willfully avoided Americanization and have favored Japanese customs, their ethnic churches and vernacular press reflect their alien orientation, and "A Jap's a Jap." Ideas of this kind were held not only by ordinary people but also by prominent and otherwise intelligent individuals. The segregated community and the minority's social solidarity undoubtedly contributed to these wildly prejudiced ideas, for anyone familiar with the Japanese minority communities and their members would have discounted such claims as unfounded. It seems clear that the majority group misperceived the activities being carried on within the communities, and the fact that the latter functioned efficiently with little reason for outside intervention added to the likelihood that they would not be understood by outsiders.

Because prejudice is an irrational thing, we do not argue that the evacuation would not have occurred if the Japanese minority community had been less segregated and less solidary. That is, under irrational conditions, any difference can be pointed to as justifying differential treatment, and no logic can undermine the justification. The only escape from this kind of vicious circle is to find means of reducing the prejudice, and ultimately that is a task for the majority group inasmuch as it is their prejudice that controls these situations. The minority group's role, however, is to do whatever it can to minimze the probability that prejudice will influence important policy decisions that may affect them.

CONTENTS

SOCIAL SOLIDARITY
AMONG THE JAPANESE IN SEATTLE

I.

INTRODUCTION

This study is an effort to present a dynamic picture of Japanese community life in America. It is a history and analysis of the Japanese community in Seattle, which may be considered a concrete case illustration of similar conditions to be found in other areas along the Pacific Coast. A conspicuous characteristic of these communities is their powerful internal solidarity, a trait of such importance in organized Japanese life as to justify special attention in this investigation.

Much already has been written concerning the Japanese in America, but the chief interest heretofore has been upon problems of immigration and Americanization, and of agitation and discrimination against these immigrants. Among existing publications one finds almost no satisfactory description of Japanese communities in America and of the day-to-day life of the people within them: their work and their play, their gains and their losses, their dreams and their anxieties, and all the compelling forces in their background determining their behavior in these activities. To understand adequately such problems as the process of Americanization or the consequence of discrimination, however, it is essential to observe the daily life of the Japanese, for the degree of their assimilation and the nature of their response to discrimination are strongly influenced by community attitudes. Thus, the need for an intimate study of the Japanese community cannot be too much emphasized.

Two further considerations point to the desirability of research on the Japanese communities in America. In the first place, these people are community-builders, or we might call them "ghetto-seekers," and they must be conceived as communities of interacting personalities rather than as aggregates of discrete individuals. The distribution of the Japanese along the Pacific Coast, for example, is primarily in concentrations about the three centers of Los Angeles, San Francisco, and Seattle.[1] Within these areas of concentration they invariably build numerous little communities. Since Japanese immigrants are seldom found adjusting to American life except in groups, to consider their problems without the relief of community background is to distort seriously the picture of their adjustment.

Another reason for emphasizing the community in a study of these immigrants is their previously indicated predisposition toward efficient community organization. As far back as 1917, when Japanese communities in America were yet comparatively in their infancy, Steiner declared:

> One of the striking characteristics of the Japanese in America is the thoroughness of their organization. . . . In their tendency to organize and in their ready response to group control, the Japanese have been equaled by few, if any, of the European groups.[2]

[1] John A. Rademaker, "Japanese Americans," *Our Racial and National Minorities,* edited by F. J. Brown and J. S. Roucek, p. 481.
[2] J. F. Steiner, *The Japanese Invasion,* p. 130.

3

Since this was written, several investigators of the Japanese in America have observed this phenomenon of group solidarity among them, and even today there seems no perceptible decrease in the solidarity of their communities.

This conception of Japanese group solidarity is no mere impression of social investigators; it has basis in facts. Juvenile delinquency rates among the Japanese, for instance, are extremely low despite their large percentage of residence within a zone of high adult criminality.[3] This fact can be explained only by assuming either that Japanese community influences are particularly favorable for their children's character, or that cases of delinquency are handled within the group. In either circumstance we have a cogent argument showing group solidarity. Again, relief agencies in Seattle seldom have Japanese names on their records, although there are cases of dependency among these immigrants. The Japanese take pride in having agencies of their own to care for such people. Yet, again, within the Japanese community there exists a whole complex of organizations and institutions to satisfy almost every social (non-economic) want of the people. Most of these institutions have been in existence for twenty years or more, and their numbers, as well as their duration of operation, indicate a wide participation in the activities of the community. It is no difficult matter to show the integrated nature of the Japanese community.

While the fact of this strong community organization among the Japanese groups in America has long been recognized, and the value of studies into the nature of their "community efficiency" has even been suggested,[4] no one, to my knowledge, has heretofore attempted any intensive investigation of Japanese communities in an effort to analyze, or even to decribe, their group solidarity.[5] It is the hope of this present study to meet what seems an inadequacy in the field of Japanese immigrant studies.

Of course, too much weight may be placed upon the factor of community organization and insufficient emphasis upon race prejudice as a reason for the solidarity of their community. Without doubt racial differences are a basic factor in keeping the Japanese and the American communities separate, but since in the past writers have overlooked to a large degree the cultural background of the Japanese, the nature of which inhibits their adjustment to the new American environment and thus gives functional significance to their community solidarity, the main attention here will be directed to a discussion of the cultural factors.

---

[3] N. S. Hayner, "Delinquency Areas in the Puget Sound Region," *American Journal of Sociology,* XXXIX (Nov. 1933), 314-328.

[4] Robert E. Park, "The Romantic Temper," *The City,* edited by Robert E. Park, Ernest W. Burgess, and Roderick D. McKenzie, pp. 121-122.

[5] See F. Fukuoka, *Mutual Life and Aid Among the Japanese in Southern California.* (Unpublished Master's thesis, University of Southern California, Los Angeles, California, 1937.) This writer treats well a limited aspect of the larger problem concerning group solidarity.

THE JAPANESE HERITAGE

One of the basic assumptions of this study is that an immigrant people interpret their new world by their old world values and attitudes. The Japanese immigrants in particular are to be understood only on the basis of this assumption, for coming as they do from a nation with a proud heritage of homogeneous culture, their national "instinct" for traditional social values tends to be far stronger than among the average national group. This fact of their cultural homogeneity, which comes from their centuries of isolation, permits a sociological analysis of their culture in brief that would otherwise be impossible; for each part of their culture is closely integrated with all the rest, and our task is simplified to that of understanding a few principles of this integration.

The essence of Japanese culture, from the standpoint of ideology, is in their ethical system—not that other cultures have no ethics, for ethics is what a group conceives as ethical, but few among the peoples of the world have made of ethics as much a conscious part of their daily lives as have the Japanese.[6] Perhaps there is no better evidence of this emphasis than that ethics is the most important requirement in every Japanese public school curriculum, and a fundamental shortcoming of the American schools from the Japanese point of view is the disregard of this subject as a daily study.

The "ethical" in the Japanese sense needs interpretation, for its meaning is different from the Occidental usage. Dr. T. Inouye clearly distinguishes between the two, where he says: "In Western ethics the dominant principle is intellectual inquiry and not the cultivation of virtue."[7] Thus, ethics for the Japanese is a practical social code applied to the regulation of daily social behavior. But we must take care not to confuse this with religious morals, as the term is used in another sense in the Occident, for among the Japanese there is nothing of supernaturalism attached to their ideas of good and evil as is common among the religious moralists of America and Europe.[8] In its simplest terms the Japanese ethical system is a set of social codes rigidly regulating the relationships of men, especially with reference to their social rank. But while this system is not basically religious, it undeniably bears the same dogmatism and the same restrictive influence.

It is difficult to show the extent to which these ethical principles permeate the whole society, but to indicate briefly: the family, for instance, must eat, yet in this most mundane experience is interwoven a series of ethical traditions, such as that the head of the family shall be served first, that food shall be offered to the dead at the family shrine, and so on. A visitor arrives, and about every exchange of greeting or remark an ethical principle is distinctly involved. A young man and woman fall in love, but between the first-felt emotion and its consummation in marriage is a host of proprieties which must be observed. In other words, for every social act there is a socially proper as well as a socially improper way, and

---

[6] Inazo Nitobe, *Bushido.*
[7] Quoted in G. B. Sansom, *Japan, a Short Cultural History,* p. 495.
[8] James S. De Benneville, *More Japonico,* pp. 78-83.

it is incumbent upon each member of this society to recognize what is the right way. In Japanese eyes society has no significance except as an interwoven whole of ethical meanings. These ethical meanings are *a priori* premises to all their social interpretations.

Understanding this fact, one may better realize the reasons for certain outstanding Japanese characteristics. Where social codes are defined in as much detail as in Japan, formalism and ceremonialism are functionally indispensible to the culture. Moreover, a vast system of etiquette, leading to an indirectness in communication and a strong awareness of social censors to individual action, are necessary. There is no need to enlarge upon the ramification of ideas that are related to their ethics, for, to put it briefly, that ramification encompasses their whole ideological system.

The primary emphasis in their ethical system is placed upon the conception of duty, or *giri* (meaning literally "right reason"),[9] a term which may be used interchangeably with "social obligation" or "social responsibility." The duties by which an individual is guided are those ideals stated centuries before by the Confucian, Buddhist and Shinto scholars. The variety of situations to which these principles apply are almost endless in extent. Thus one may speak of duties to oneself, to one's parents and family, to the neighbors, the community, the nation— and the supreme duty of all, to one's emperor. From the requirements of duty follow other ethical conceptions such as sacrifice, honor, loyalty, and courage. We may perhaps well understand the severity of the Japanese nation; a people driven by the stern command of duty are not a people given to mildness of action. Duty, or the conception of social responsibility, is therefore the dynamic focus of the Japanese ethical system.

If we look for a concrete expression of this ideology in the social organization of the Japanese, we find that their family system, and its basal cult of ancestor worship, are integrally related to their ethical principles. In Japan the family rather than the individual is the unit of society, and every member of a family feels a sense of responsibility to the rest. Control is vested in the hands of the male head, and his authority, within limits of reason and tradition, leaves no room for questioning from subordinate members. Hence, to have a son or daughter sue the parents in a law court, as sometimes happens in America, would be unthinkable in Japan. The Japanese conception of the family is not limited, as a rule, to the household. There is a constant tendency for primary-group attitudes to reach beyond the limits of one's legal kinsfolk and apply to the largest unit conceivable as a family. Such a unit in Japanese conception takes in the nation, for from a historical point of view the people consider themselves all of one blood. It may be observed that the foundation of this organization is the ethical system of collective obligations, and it is this which gives the Japanese family a type of solidarity hardly to be conceived in the Western mind.

---

[9] Note the similarity of this to the emphasis upon duty in the ethical philosophy of Emmanuel Kant. It is perhaps no accident that the Japanese feel a strong admiration for the German people, the nation that produced the great Kant.

Having described their ethical code and their family organization, we are now in a position to trace out other facets of their culture pattern. We can understand their acceptance of authoritarianism and the development of inhibition, reserve, non-inventiveness and imitativeness under this conformance to discipline. We can take their emphasis upon honor, ambition, service and recognition, and fit it all into the larger pattern. However, the endless ramifications of this pattern need not be indicated, for the description which has been given here sufficiently suggests the general leaning of the Japanese mind.

It now remains for us to interpret this background description for its significance in understanding Japanese community solidarity.

Central in the Japanese social organization, we have said, is the code of duties that defines the roles and obligations of the members of that society. The authority that enforces these obligations is the Japanese belief in the superiority and the greater importance of the group over the individual.[10] Among the Japanese, therefore, solidarity is maintained by forcing individuals to conform with the traditional group values, while potential recalcitrants are kept in line by social opinion that is weighted with the freight of traditional ethical views.

Where development of personality is thus restricted by strong authoritarianism, and where, indeed, it is virtuous to act in conformance with traditional social behavior, there is little of the individualism so highly idealized in American society. It is understandable why the Japanese cannot appreciate the American lack of respect towards authority, for while the Americans place their premium upon experimentalism, the Japanese feel a higher regard for conformism. In so far as Japanese group solidarity is concerned it is well that there is this conformity, for as soon as the members break from tradition and become individualistic, they sever the bonds which hold them together.

In our description of Japanese culture, too, we have suggested the strong awareness which the Japanese feel for the reality of the group. The family, the community, and even so large a unit as the nation, have a reality more concrete than even the individual person. They feel this unity because the whole of their culture is integrated like a mosaic, and has a certain harmony throughout from the largest to the smallest cultural unit. They feel its concreteness because all of their history, art, religion, and education emphasizes symbolisms of the group.

Finally, we may note the sacredness with which the Japanese view their social world, for their whole ethical system, based as it is upon doctrines that have been handed down through long historical tradition, and reinforced by unquestioning sanctions through centuries, has come to have the incontestable authority of the Mosaic Laws. There is, perhaps, no supernaturalism in the Japanese attitudes toward these codes, but the Japanese are as certain of the rationality of the codes as if they were of divine origin. Such is their authoritarianism, tested by the weathering of time and become so deeply rooted that none may now question it. Because the code that it dictates is sacred in the minds of the Japanese, any-

---

[10] This is Emile Durkheim's position as stated in *La division du travail social,* 1896.

one who fails to live in accordance with it sins as deeply as does the religious heretic who denies a god.

This is the heritage which the Japanese brought with them when they arrived on the American shores,[11] and what there is in the community that is strange to the American eye must be interpreted in the light of this background. We have seen that the collectivistic system of Japan gave a strong base to group solidarity. What the effects were of transplanting this system upon a new soil, we may observe in the following discussion.

---

[11] It is true that the industrial Japan of today differs in many respects from the relatively feudal Japanese culture described here, but for most of the Japanese immigrants in America, coming as they did in the early 1900's, the latter is their heritage, and these are the traditions they have attempted to preserve. As Ichihashi once remarked, "If one wants to study the Japan of thirty years ago, he could not do better than to investigate some of the Japanese communities existent in America today."

II.

BACKGROUNDS TO THE COMMUNITY

Almost directly to the southeast of Seattle's central business district in the gargantuan shadows of the Smith Tower are several streets of small shops occupied by busy little dark-skinned men. Here, near Fifth and Sixth avenues on Main and Jackson streets, is the business center of the Japanese district, consisting of a congeries of shops including everything from barber shops and restaurants to book stores and law offices. The business center is not today what it was in the heyday of the early nineteen-twenties, when Main Street really teemed with the life of incoming immigrants and prosperous farmers visiting town. Rather is one aware now that the depression has not dealt kindly with these shop-keepers; that the failure of the community's one bank, and the large movements of their population back to Japan, and even more to California, have drained a good part of the life-blood out of the community.

When one climbs up First Hill just to the east of this business area, one sees but the semblance of what once was the main residential area of the immigrant Japanese. The Japanese unquestionably continue here in large numbers, but one is impressed today more with the increasing number of old frame houses that are dark and hollow with their vacancy. The movement of life seems to have slowed to the pace of the "Skidroad" bum wandering up the hill, with a dollar rubbing his limb deep in his pocket, occasionally stopping uncertainly before a house where a rap on the window calls attention to the lewd wares of an illegitimate commerce.

And yet, because the community is not as visible today as it once was, it is not to be assumed that it no longer exists. It is true that one needs to wander farther to the east, past these houses now beyond repair, to find the Japanese scattered out on other hillsides mingling with the Jews, the Italians and other working-class whites. If one troubles to spot their residences on a map, the picture appears like a target bespattered by a bad marksman, for the dots show in all parts of the city. Still, in a real sense the community continues at the center, for it is from here that the bonds of community solidarity are drawn.

This center runs from Yesler Way southward to Dearborn, and from First Avenue eastward to Sixteenth, and for all its apparent loss of vigor, it is within this area or on the fringe of it that almost all the important Japanese institutions still tend to be congregated. It is into this area, too, that the Japanese pour whenever any event of importance among them occurs, whether it be the celebration of a Japanese holiday or the carrying on of an athletic affair.

By the term Japanese community, therefore, it is possible to refer to two distinct aspects of it. The one is the totality of Japanese living within the civic boundaries of Seattle who feel a common bond with all the rest of their nation-

9

ality; the other is the central area within which all of their major activities are carried on. In this study we are thinking of the total community, for it is the solidarity of this aggregate which is significant. There was a day when these two communities were not distinct, and since it is in the immigrants' memories and sentiments about those yesteryears that one finds reasons for the way they feel about the community as it stands today, the story of its growth, however brief, needs to be told.

Although early historical accounts about the Japanese immigrants to this section of the United States are incomplete, there are reports of thirty-four Japanese working in the Northwest as early as 1878. It was not until 1890 that a few of them began to operate their own small enterprises, and by 1900 a noticeable group had assembled in this incipient community.[1] From then on the growth of the community was rapid, though their history was marked by critical events.

Among the most significant events influencing the growth of the community were certain international crises and movements, and the striking manner in which they have directed the history of this community justifies special emphasis upon them in our interpretation of the community's development. These events were: (1) the expanding economy of Japan, markedly noticeable by 1900; (2) the signing of the Gentlemen's Agreement in 1907; (3) the World War and the resulting war boom; and (4) the passage of the Anti-Alien Land Laws and the Immigration Act of 1924.

By their conquest of the Chinese in 1895, and the foothold which they consequently gained on the mainland, the Japanese nation was experiencing about 1900 a very definite economic as well as psychological expansion. Their dreams of adventure and advance in wealth and status went far beyond anything ever conceived before. But the lower economic classes, since they lacked capital, were frustrated in their desire to participate in this general expansion. It is not surprising, therefore, that this group, who saw little opportunity in their native land, who were eager for adventure and who had heard tales of the great wealth in America, looked hopefully to this country. For these immigrants America was a land of opportunity where they might quickly accumulate wealth, but it was also only a step to the higher goal which they sought, namely, status in their own land. Hence, they came willing to work at anything which would permit them to save, whether as railroad section hands, as sawmill hands, or as domestic servants, for in the longer perspective they dreamed of prestige and comfort in their homeland.[2]

It was by good chance that the Japanese came to Seattle about that time, for the city itself as a frontier community was in the throes of expansion. Building and commerce were going forward at an unusual rate, and there were not enough workers to go around. The whites were glad of the small services provided by the little Orientals, and there were few to reject them at the time. The wages for their work, it is true, were low; too low, in fact, to permit sufficient savings for their

---

[1] For a detailed history of the Japanese in Seattle see *Nippon Immin-Shi,* edited by K. Takeuchi.

[2] Document SX5. (All document references are to statements made by persons in the community in personal interviews. Names are withheld for obvious reasons.)

return to Japan as they at first had planned. But many did well, and none were without work.[3]

This may be called the "frontier period" of the community, for it bore all the traits characteristic of the frontier. The population was composed largely of laboring-class males, almost all of whom were "birds of passage" eager to make quick money and return to Japan. Families were few, and only the bare framework of the institutional organization necessary for the wants of a normal community was existent. The immigrants found their residences near what is now lower Jackson Street and the "Skidroad" area, for here the rents were cheapest, and their services of restaurants, barber shops, and hotels were sought by the working-class whites living near there.

The signing of the Gentlemen's Agreement in 1907 signalized a shift in the attitude of the community. It is probable that the Japanese in Seattle were themselves highly sensitive to the criticism, implied in the Agreement, against the frontier aspects of their community, as witness their self-motivated action in cleaning out the colony of Japanese prostitutes.[4] Furthermore, though with the passing years the first hopes of "getting-rich-quick" and returning home were banished, each year of life here made adjustments easier and more congenial. Consequently, the early eagerness and urge to get back to Japan became less active. Lastly, the Gentlemen's Agreement altered the type of immigrants to this community, and a stabler element than had heretofore been present was introduced.[5] The result was a shift from the "frontier period" of the community to what might be called a "settling period."

A new lease of interest was created in building up the community. Families were emphasized, and problems of marriage arose. New institutions were necessitated to bridge the gap for the settling Japanese immigrants between their native heritage and the American environment. In short, a definite trend towards the establishment of a ghetto was apparent.

The "settling period" entered into another phase, however, with the coming of the World War, especially following the entry of the United States into the conflict. The great ship-building activity that this brought to Seattle also brought in its train a flood of workers and maximum wages. For the Japanese this meant a great demand for all their small services of hotels, dye works, and restaurants, while the Japanese farmers reached a peak on their crop prices. The effect upon the community was electric. There was an unprecedented expansion of business, an increased inflow of immigrants, and the expanding mood was evidenced even in their ecological distribution which, like a congested bud blooming forth in the sunshine of the day, showed the Japanese moving out into areas they had not dared to enter before. One wonders what the effect of this movement would have been upon the solidarity of the community in the long run had not other critical events followed.

---

[3]Document SX8.
[4]See page 31.
[5]Y. Ichihashi, *Japanese in the United States*, p. 69.

The events to which I refer are the signing of the Anti-Alien Land Law in 1921 for the state of Washington, and the passage of the Immigration Act in 1924. By the first enactment foreign-born Japanese could no longer lease or own land. The consequent disruption of the Japanese farming community in the Puget Sound Region dealt a serious blow to the Japanese business men of Seattle who counted in no small degree upon the trade of these farmers. This, coupled with a gradual decline in the value of farm products upon the market, became a threat to the Japanese business community in Seattle.

The Immigration Act of 1924 was an even more serious blow, for by its passage the further immigration of the Japanese to this country was prohibited. As a result, a community geared economically to expect a constant inflow of immigrants found its organization stranded, and the community had to alter its economic structure radically. Second, by the decline in the community's economic base, and the blow to its pride, a gap was made between the Japanese and their white neighbors; and third, the period of establishing families was ended. As the first-generation Japanese saw the visions of their future opportunities more and more restricted, a new emphasis was placed upon the second (American-born) generation who by virtue of their birthright could have that which the first generation could not possess. It is from this last emphasis that we take the name for this last period, and call the years from 1924 up to the present the "second-generation" period.

By reason of its peculiar history, therefore, which certain legal restrictions and international crises had a direct effect in shaping, the Japanese community in Seattle today bears characteristics which a normal growth would not have brought out.

In the ecological organization of the community, for example, certain consequences of community history are evident. A spot map of the population distribution in 1912 shows an extreme concentration of Japanese within an area of several blocks surrounding their business center near Sixth Avenue and Main Street.[6] Almost no scatter of their population into other parts of the city is abservable, and this is explained by their relatively recent entry into the "settling period." Yet the community's tendency to creep eastward along Yesler Way and Jackson Street was already noticeable. The pattern of population distribution for both the Chinese and the Japanese during these earlier years was similar, but has become divergent with the passage of time. The Chinese tend to continue in their highly concentrated community, no doubt due to their lack of families here, while the Japanese show distinctly their tendency towards what may be called a "bursting" type of distribution.[7]

This "bursting" distribution is in evidence by 1920 (Figure I), for though we find the heaviest concentration of spots still at the center, the number of residents scattered in the outlying areas gives an indication of their surprising mobility over a relatively short period of eight years. These were the years of the

---

[6] John A. Rademaker, *Ecological Distribution of the Japanese and Chinese in Seattle.* (Unpublished manuscript.)
[7] *Ibid.*

war boom, and the Japanese were enjoying its fruits. Not only were they able, with their increased income, to seek out better homes than the ones provided in the central district, but they found their small-shop services welcomed by the white working class in areas other than the "Skidroad" district.[8] A former operator of a hotel comments:

> The outward movement of the Japanese hotels came during the war-times, for it was then that a great demand for rooms was created among the ship-workers and others who flooded this town. These workers were, in the main, single men, and hotel rooms were much desired by them.[9]

This was a time of ecological expansion, and one wonders whether there might not have been a concomitant psychological expansion; whether if, in those years, the Japanese did not find the Americans to be an amiable people, a people with whom they should have desired to assimilate. Had that period of prosperity and interracial congeniality continued, what would have been the effect upon Japanese community solidarity?—but this is a question that can never be answered.

A study of the ecological distribution in 1930 and 1935 shows consequences of the Immigration Act of 1924 in the thinning out that takes place at the center of the community (Figures II and III)*. With a ban placed upon the further entry of Japanese immigrants into Seattle, the population that normally would have recruited the center failed to materialize. Furthermore, the older immigrants, with increased adaptation to the American community, and larger incomes with which to buy and rent homes in the better residential areas, quit the central district. Our map, in consequence, shows the Japanese rather evenly scattered over a large part of the city.

But, as I have earlier indicated, in spite of these movements of population into white communities, their relation with the whites is still essentially symbiotic, and their orientation remains toward the Japanese community. Just to what extent anti-Japanese legislation has been responsible for this retardation of assimilation we can only conjecture. While it is likely that the traditional Japanese heritage is basic in the persistence of this orientation toward their native culture, the anti-Japanese agitations were also an important factor in determining this orientation as is indicated by the following statement from one of the older immigrants:

> I still feel a longing to go back to Japan. Here in this country, I am an alien because I have no citizenship, and my world feels small because it is restricted at certain points. When I walk around among the Americans, I have a feeling that I don't belong here. But back in Japan I would be in a position to do things as I want to, to help in the operation of the government.[10]

Not only in the spatial distribution of the population, but even more markedly in the composition of the population do we have evidence of the historical influence. Some of the basic influences are seen by a study of Table I which indi-

---

*Figures I, II, and III, pp. 35, 36, 37.

[8] A comparison of the addresses of hotels, groceries, and dye works between 1916 and 1920 gives vivid evidence of the ecological expansion of the small shops. See *North American Times Year Book* for 1916 and 1920.

[9] Document SX5.

[10] Document SX8.

cates the growth of the Japanese population in Seattle since 1900. Most obvious among these changes is the very rapid proportional decline of the foreign-born

TABLE I

JAPANESE POPULATION OF SEATTLE BY NATIVITY FROM 1900 TO 1930[11]

Year	Total	NATIVE-BORN		FOREIGN-BORN	
		No.	Per cent	No.	Per cent
1900............................	2,990	.....	..	.....	..
1910............................	6,127	378	6	5,749	94
1920............................	7,874	1,863	24	6,011	76
1930............................	8,448	4,000	47	4,448	53

[11] U. S. Census, 1930, Vol. III, part 2, Table XXVII, p. 1231.

between 1910 and 1930, and especially between 1920 and 1930. The latter, of course, is a direct result of the immigration ban. The important fact to note is the rapidity with which the community is becoming dominated numerically by the native-born population, for if this trend continues, which is most likely, the old Japanese traits which have been effective in preserving community solidarity in the past are likely, in the future, to become weaker.

The cleavage between the two generations, the distinctly bimodal character of their age distribution, is even more strikingly brought out in the population pyramid of the Japanese in Seattle for 1935 (Figure IV.)* The cleavage which this graph illustrates is not merely statistical; it is present in the actual life of the people. Just as the top-heavy first-generation group in the pyramid rests heavily upon the second-generation base, so likewise do they dominate the life of the community in so far as authority is concerned. Just as the one is placed on an entirely different level than the other in the diagram, so in actual life do they tend to live in two different worlds, neither understanding, literally or figuratively, the language of the other. And just as the older group climb closer to the peak of the pyramid of the Japanese in Seattle for 1935 (Figure IV)*. The cleavage which the full vigor of their life. Yet, for the present at least, despite their growing age, control is essentially in the hands of the first generation, and the institutions which frame the life of the community continue mainly after their patterning.

It is for this reason that our discussion will be restricted mainly to the first generation, and their part in giving solidarity to the community. It is recognized that the role played by the second-generation Japanese in bringing about community solidarity may thus be unduly minimized, but the limits of this thesis will not permit an adequate treatment of the second-generation group.[12]

In this chapter an attempt has been made to point out the orientation of the community, whether towards Japan or towards America, and the reasons for it.

---

*Figure IV, p. 38.

[12] For a detailed study of the second generation and their relation to the Japanese community, see Forrest LaViolette, *Types of Adjustment among Second-Generation Japanese* (unpublished doctor's thesis, University of Chicago, Chicago, in preparation).

In the basic orientation of the Japanese community—in their tendency to look towards Japan—we have an explanation, in part, of their community solidarity. Had these Japanese discarded their heritage of a collectivistic tradition, in the thirty years and more of their residence here, and accepted America more fully, it is doubtful if their community solidarity would be what it is today. Their historical background was of such nature that they could not leave the bosom of their community and cast off their ties completely. There was a period when they might have broken away, but subsequent events drove them back.

On the other hand, in the rising importance of the second-generation group we have the portent of a break from these ancient collectivistic traditions, and it would seem from a study of the population pyramid that when the break comes it will come suddenly. Even as I describe the community in these pages, the changes taking place are so rapid that the attitudes discussed here are being outmoded. But, on the other hand, as LaViolette's study of the second generation seems to indicate, the degree to which this group conforms to the Japanese traditions is considerably more than is observable on the surface, and in so far as this is so, this study provides an important background for an understanding of the second-generation personality pattern.

III.

COMMUNITY INSTITUTIONS AND SOLIDARITY

Institutions, since they are more concrete and objective than attitudes, for example, are particularly useful as objects of sociological study. Moreover, since they are the carriers of those group values which have been crystallized out in a society, institutions are a good criterion, in themselves, of the group's way of thinking about things. Japanese community solidarity is at bottom a product of their way of thinking about their world, and since Japanese institutions are particularly convenient for studying, and since they hold within their organization the Japanese group attitudes that give foundation to their solidarity, they have been chosen as the objects of this study.

We shall begin with a consideration of the economic institutions in the community, for in the way that men buy and sell are often revealed some of the most poignant facts about a given cultural pattern.

Economic Institutions

Since conceptions of ethics, and particularly conceptions of collective obligations, are central in the Japanese view of their society, we should expect to see these applied in their economic activities as well. In this section we shall attempt to demonstrate how attitudes of mutual responsibility made possible the building up of such an economic organization as exists today, and what their effects were in bringing about community solidarity. We shall observe certain seeds of disorganization, however, in the Japanese effort to apply primary-group attitudes to the secondary-group relationships characteristic of American economic life.

In speaking of the economic activities of the Japanese in Seattle, we must take special note of the overwhelming dominance in their lives of the "small shop." Five per cent of the gainfully employed in America, Lewis Corey tells us, come from that group which he labels the "small independent entrepreneur,"[1] but among the Seattle Japanese 46 per cent of the income earners are those with an independent small business (independent professionals such as lawyers, doctors, and photographers are included in this group in accordance with Corey's classification). Moreover, another 25 per cent are stenographers, clerks, teachers, salesmen and public officials, whose interests are essentially related to those entrepreneurs because they are directly dependent upon them. Of the remaining 19 per cent, a large portion are porters, domestic servants, drivers, and seasonal workers, making up an obviously nondescript group somewhat different from the usual composition of the working class.[2]

---

[1] Lewis Corey, *The Crisis of the Middle Class*, p. 156.
[2] Computed from the figures of *The Seattle Japanese Occupational Census, 1935,* published by the Seattle Japanese Chamber of Commerce.

There is an area of economic, as well as of social, life belonging to the *kaisha* group (people who work for the local branches of large corporations in Japan) that is entirely distinct from the life of the small business men, but since the former are a group who are transferred at the will of the companies and do not take deep roots in the community, the problem of their relation to the local group must be considered as outside the scope of this present study.

Thus, when we note the lack of any capitalist or upper-middle class in this community,[3] and when we see the vagueness and the relative smallness of a true working class, we can understand the remarkable predominance of a single class-interest. Indeed, in talking to the people in the community, one feels the absence of class consciousness at least on the basis of wealth, among them, and a reporter on a Japanese newspaper to whom I put the question of class divisions had, at first, difficulty in understanding what I meant.[4]

Not only is there identity of class interests, but there is an even greater identity of occupational interests. A study of the occupational classification of the Japanese in Seattle discloses that 45 per cent of the workers fall under the category of "trades." Of the 31 per cent classed under "domestic and personal services," 29 per cent are included under hotels, restaurants, barber shops, and laundries (Table II). The latter, however, are occupations so similar to the trades that it is difficult to distinguish the two. Rightly speaking, they may all be listed under one occupational group.

TABLE II

OCCUPATIONAL CLASSIFICATION OF THE JAPANESE IN SEATTLE, 1935

Occupation	MALE		FEMALE		TOTAL	
	No.	%	No.	%	No.	%
Agriculture	94	4	2	0	96	3
Clerical	91	4	31	5	122	4
Domestic and Personal Service	627	27	259	46	886	31
Extraction of Mineral	1	0	0	0	1	0
Forestry and Fishing	11	0	0	0	11	0
Manufacturing & Mechanical Indus	83	4	73	13	156	6
Professional Service	123	5	56	10	179	6
Public Service	55	2	0	0	55	2
Trade	1,146	50	146	26	1,292	45
Transportation and Communication	69	4	0	0	69	3
TOTAL	2,300	100	567	100	2,867	100

[3] One man, prior to the depression, might have been included in this category, but the failure of his bank during the crisis ended his economic dominance.

[4] There is some confusion among the people of the community as to what is the basis of class differentiation. In the past, status has been determined by the amount of social service rendered by the individual to society. However, the tendency to distinguish classes on the basis of economic success is becoming more prominent. It is probable that this attitude would have been more prevalent in the community today had there developed a greater economic differentiation.

Yet to say that 74 per cent are in trades still does not adequately picture the breadth of common occupational interests among these tradespeople. Their closely integrated economic interests stand out more clearly when we list the ten most important trades among the Japanese, and discover the large number of establishments included under each:[5]

TABLE III

TEN MOST IMPORTANT TRADES AMONG THE JAPANESE IN SEATTLE, 1935

Trades	No. of Establishments
Hotels	183
Groceries	148
Dye works	94
Public-market stands	64
Produce houses	57
Gardeners	42
Restaurants	36
Barber shops	36
Laundries	31
Peddlers (fruit and vegetables)	24

In a restricted community such as that of the Japanese in Seattle, when twenty-five or more persons enter the same occupation, it is inevitable that a certain identity of interest is built up among them, and that this identity of interest goes beyond the mere economic sphere of their lives.[6]

Here, in the similarity of their economic interests, is a major factor in the solidarity of this group but to understand how the solidification came about, one must comprehend the interplay, within their economic activities, of traditional Japanese attitudes about collective obligation.

For instance, some of the points raised by the foregoing data need clarification. How did all of these immigrants, with a very inadequate background in these trades, learn them sufficiently well to be successful in establishing and promoting their individual enterprises? How did they finance themselves in establishing these enterprises, and in expanding them? Why did not the community proceed to break up when the entrepreneurs began to expand out into the white-American community?

We may begin our inquiry by considering how the Japanese first established themselves in the trades.

Like most immigrant people coming to America, the Japanese immigrants were mainly from a farming and laboring class background, and had little business training. Despite these circumstances, however, they seem not to have been deterred by their primary inadequacies from setting up their individual trades.

---

[5] *Seattle Japanese Occupational Census of 1935,* published by the Seattle Japanese Chamber of Commerce.

[6] See also Table IV for detailed account of Japanese occupations in Seattle in 1930.

BUSINESS CENSUS OF SEATTLE JAPANESE COMUNITY – DEC. 1930

COMPILED BY: Miyamoto and Sakima

BUSINESS	INVEST-MENT	YEARLY INCOME
PHYSICIAN	$55,000	$60,000
PRINTING SHOP	30,000	57,000
FLORIST	28,000	130,000
HAT CLEANING	2,000	18,000
HOTEL	1,814,578	1,643,250
INSURANCE AGENT	35,000	
BOTTLE SUPPLY STORE	30,000	76,000
LAWYER	1,400	
BAKERY	12,500	60,000
WATCH REPAIR	81,500	111,500
DRY-GOOD STORE	90,000	294,918
BARBER SHOP	92,400	177,500
JAPANESE RESTAURANT	134,300	372,500
HARDWARE STORE	26,250	45,340
ROOMING HOUSE	17,000	32,050
GREEN HOUSE	140,000	49,000
BOND BROKER	70,000	170,000
SHOE REPAIR	30,000	96,000
TAXI SERVICE	30,000	30,000
PAPER-BAG STORE	8,500	10,000
PAPER HANGER	6,000	6,000
MOTION-PICTURE THEATER	45,000	90,000
FURNITURE STORE	153,000	290,000
CANDY STORE	26,000	58,000
TAILOR	91,400	164,610
AMERICAN RESTAURANT	187,000	1,388,000
EGG DEALER	2,000	10,000
POOL HALL	9,000	35,200
DYE WORK	273,000	287,000
CARPENTRY	2,000	3,200
TIRE SHOP	10,000	28,500
NOODLE SHOP	13,500	32,900
SOFT DRINK	24,300	60,100
FISHING TACKLE	40,000	40,000
INTERPRETOR	13,800	19,800
CHIROPRACTOR		
FISH-DEALER	188,250	1,375,300
EXPRESS AGENCY	18,000	20,100
PRODUCE HOUSE	109,350	1,054,278
VEGETABLE MARKET	248,000	910,000
VEGETABLE VENDER	244,800	61,100
GROCERY	486,500	3,560,500
GARAGE	48,000	100,440
DRUG STORE	284,500	190,400
EMPLOYMENT AGENCY	3,000	6,000
REAL ESTATE DEALER	17,850	17,500
PLUMBER	5,500	27,000
FERMENTED RICE STORE	7,700	3,190
SECOND-HAND STORE	75,000	144,988
RAILROAD WORKER CONTRACT	122,000	1,330,134
ELECTRICAL APPLIANCE	19,500	22,400
IRON WORKS	2,500	5,000
SIGN PAINTING	1,800	5,000
CANNERY CONTRACTOR	212,000	530,122
BANK	430,000	
IMPORT & EXPORT DEALER	788,500	7,733,831
PUBLIC BATH HOUSE	16,250	29,700
MEAT MARKET	41,000	121,600
PAWN BROKER	75,000	32,500
BOOK STORE	48,000	35,000
DENTIST	74,400	67,200
PHOTOGRAPHER	35,000	34,000
PROVISION MFG.	68,000	78,000
MIDWIFE	1,025	7,900
TEN-CENT STORE	50,250	60,200
JUNK DEALER	1,500	2,500
ANTIQUE SHOP	13,000	33,000
BEAUTY SHOP	5,000	14,000
LAUNDRY	144,136	283,120
SWEATER MFG.	25,000	40,000
KAISHA		
TOTAL	7,775,559	24,055,684

TABLE IV

For one thing, the practice of establishing individual enterprises is something traceable to Japan. As one business man put it:

> There's a custom in Japan which you won't find in America, that a man who has worked for another for a long time will eventually be financed by his employer in starting a branch office of his own. In other words, it's natural that everyone should own his individual shop.[7]

The tradition of individual enterprise was, therefore, well laid in the customs of Japan. Though a large percentage of the immigrants were from rural areas, the growing impetus of westernization and industrialization encouraged the development in the country districts of favorable attitudes toward town trades.[8] Despite what may be said of Japan's rapid adaptation to Western culture, the Japan of the early 1900's was still relatively close to her feudal background, and the Japanese immigrants of that day, for all their compulsion to enter the city trades, were almost totally unfamiliar with American trade habits and tastes.

There were, of course, certain favoring circumstances that facilitated this early period of adjustment, and we get a very clear picture of all this in a statement by an old-time immigrant who describes the manner in which the Japanese first established themselves in the restaurant service.

> These Japanese came here with nothing but a blanket on their back—they had no money, they didn't know any English, they didn't know how to do any of the things that the Americans know, nor how the Americans made their living—so they had to start from the bottom. But, of course, the restaurant cooking of that day was relatively simple; all one had to know was how to fry an egg, toast bread, and fry a steak. It was known as "fry cook." Mr. T. was the first to get started in that line of business. And then other Japanese worked in his place, learned the trade, and started businesses of their own. They catered to the many laborers who lived down near the lower end of the city at the time, and they did very well, for the white men found these lunch-counter services cheap and convenient.[9]

Similar conditions held for other trades as well. It was primarily by trial and error that these first immigrants learned their trades, and since in the "frontier period" there were large demands for the services of these tradesmen, and the tastes of their customers were not fastidious, it was possible for them to adjust satisfactorily to their new work. In later years, on the other hand, when the trades became more complex, the novice was able to profit by the experiences of those who had preceded him, and, in fact, a tendency grew for tradesmen to draw into their own occupational field those who were their closest friends.

The influence of prefectural groups, known as *ken-jin*,[10] in this connection of attracting in-group members, is well illustrated in the following statement:

> There was a tendency towards the concentration of people from the same prefectures in Japan at the same places, and in the same lines of work. For example, the barbers in Seattle, at least in the old days, all tended to be people from the Yamaguchi-*ken*, for Mr. I. came first and established himself in that line, and then helped his friends from Japan to get started. Then again, in the restaurant business, the majority of them are *Ehime-ken*, for men like Mr. K. first got into this, and

---

[7] Document SX5.

[8] G. B. Sansom, *op. cit.,* p. 514.

[9] Document SX8.

[10] *Ken-jin* is literally translated as "prefectural person." A *ken*, or prefecture, is comparable to the state in this country. Hence, to speak of a Yamaguchi-*kenjin* is comparable to speaking, for instance, of an Iowan.

then aided his *ken* friends to follow in the same field. Homes like those of Mr. I.
were places of congregation for the young men who were eager to learn things and
to discuss them, and in the course of their association learned such trades as their
friends knew.[11]

Thus, in the learning of their trades, the gaps in the immigrant's knowledge
were bridged through the aid of circumstances and of friends, but the problem of
financing their enterprises had no such ready solution.

It is true that most Japanese immigrants started their business on the savings
made after first working in sawmills or on railways, but few among them were
able to expand their business individually to any great extent. Possibly without a
system of cooperative financing the Japanese would not have developed the economic structure that they did. Fortunately, they met their needs through adaptations of Japanese customs, such as a money-pool known as the *tanomoshi*. (The
literal translation of the word is "to rely on, or depend upon.")

Briefly, the *tanomoshi* operates in this manner. If some individual, whom
we shall call A, needs monetary aid, he calls upon one of his close friends, B, to
start a *tanomoshi*. B then goes around to several of their common friends and in-
duces a group of fifteen or twenty who are interested in such a *tanomoshi* to
gather at a dinner on an appointed date. Each contributes an agreed sum, such as
$25 or $50, and the pool is rented to A *gratis* since the object of it is primarily to
help him. A ordinarily reciprocates by paying the cost of the dinner, and he later
pays off his obligations with a small monetary gift to each of the members. His
debt is paid back in monthly installments. Thereafter, monthly meetings are called
in which new pools are set up, and the remaining members bid for its use, the bid
representing the interest upon the principal which the individuals agree to pay.
With the passing of each monthly meeting, the circle of bidders is gradually nar-
rowed down.[12] The *tanomoshi* closes when each member has paid his debt. This,
of course, is only one form of the *tanomoshi,* since several variations are possible.[18]

It is difficult to ascertain the extent to which such pools were used by the
Japanese immigrants to aid their economic circumstances, but from the widespread recognition of its use, it was probably no inconsequential part of their financing practices. The largest hotel enterprise ever attempted by the Japanese, a
transaction involving some $90,000, which later failed, was financed on the basis
of a *tanomoshi*.

More significant than the novelty of the *tanomoshi*, however, is the function
which it serves. We must note that the *tanomoshi* is called, in the first place, to
help a friend who is in need of financial aid; that the *tanomoshi* meetings must be
dinner affairs, signifying their importance as a social function; that the method
of auctioning is used to enhance the spirit of the gathering; that the interest pay-
ments are called gifts (honorable politenesses) rather than by their true commercial name, and that small lotteries are usually held on the side to add further so-

[11] Document SX8.
[12] Document SX1.
[18] Gunther Stein, "Made in Japan," *Forum Magazine*. November 1935, Vol. XCIV, p. 292.

cial interest to the meeting. A most important fact, also, is that no security is demanded of the members other than their own good name, although today the security of the "good name" seems to have decreased considerably in value. No better illustration than this can be given of the Japanese tendency to project primary-group attitudes into such secondary-group relations as commercial transactions which in the American community are ordinarily thoroughly rationalized and impersonalized.

We may briefly summarize, then, the factors which were basic in leading these Japanese immigrants into the field of the "small shop." First, as we have seen, there existed a tradition in the culture background of the people towards their entry into this field. Second, there was in Japan an expanding economy which predisposed these migrants to set up individual enterprises, while on their arrival in Seattle they found an expanding frontier community wholly willing to accept a new immigrant group that would offer them much-needed small shop services. Finally, these immigrants had in their mores traditional practices of mutual aid that shortly became institutionalized in the *kenjinkai* and the *tanomoshi*, and enabled the pooling of funds essential to the growth of all their numerous businesses.

It is possible to see how feelings of group solidarity grew out of this interplay in the attitudes of collective responsibility during these years of establishment. From the Japanese point of view one good turn always demands another in return, and the net effect of these extensive mutual assistances was a tightening of the community bonds. Yet not alone in the interaction among the Japanese themselves, but as well in their relationship with the larger community surrounding them, were factors of solidarity in operation. The solidification that followed certain anti-Japanese agitations gives vivid evidence of this tendency.

The earliest developments in the economic organization of the Japanese took place in the central district of their community. Quite early, however, seekers for greater profits tended to move outward with such businesses as hotels, dyeworks, produce-houses, markets, and restaurants, in which they frequently came into direct competition with American entrepreneurs. The result was anti-Japanese agitation in which the tactics used by the Americans in their efforts to quash this Japanese invasion lay in threats of boycott against any wholesalers who sold goods to the Japanese.

But as Sumner points out, "Nothing so easily establishes solidarity within a group as an attack from without." The Japanese had latent within the community all the forces enabling quick mobilization of their members into such groups as their business associations. Therefore, these attempts to drive out the Japanese were never successful, for the Japanese themselves formed associations and returned the fight by threats of boycott against any who refused to sell to their people. These threats were made effective by promising certain wholesale houses having large Japanese trade the concentration of all Japanese business with them if they would continue their sale of goods. It was never impossible to find the weakest link in the line of boycotters and every effort to drive them out failed.

While the main function of these business associations was to facilitate the relationships between the Japanese business men and the white community, the social function of these organizations was hardly less important. In almost all cases, these organizations were first formed to provide some social outlet for the members and to promote good-will and friendship among them. The effect of attacks from outside was merely to crystallize these loose bonds. Today there are twenty-two of these business associations organized under the dominance of the Seattle Japanese Chamber of Commerce.[14]

While business associations have long been well received within the community, cooperatives, contrary to the belief of some investigators of the Japanese have never been wholly successful. During the depression, when the prices received by the farmers and by the produce men on Western Avenue were at their lowest, enterprising leaders in that business felt a need for some cooperative association to better regulate the prices at the market. The idea was agreed to be excellent, and a movement was put under way to establish such a cooperative, but the attempt eventually failed. One member of this organization who had an important part in its leadership explained the difficulty in this way:

> The trouble with the Japanese is that they always want to make themselves look good on the front, but their business on the inside is just a mess. For one thing, most of these farmers had been borrowing from the American firms, and they were obliged to take their produce to those companies to whom they owed money. Many of them had a little debt here, and a little debt there, and they were just tied hand and foot. In a cooperative, it's necessary that everybody show their hands, and lay down all their cards on the table. But the Japanese won't do that, and for that reason the Cooperative has been very difficult to operate.[15]

The failure to cooperate seems a contradiction of the analysis which we have made thus far of Japanese economic solidarity, but in reality the contradiction serves to clarify our foregoing explanations. In order to make my point clear it is necessary to recognize, as Margaret Mead has done in her recent book *Cooperation and Competition Among Primitive Peoples,* the distinction between cooperation and helpfulness. She says:

> In cooperation, the goal is shared and it is the relationship to the goal which holds the cooperating individuals together; in helpfulness, the goal is shared only through the relationship of the helpers to the individual whose goal it actually is.[16]

The Japanese are quite obviously not cooperative, at least in the realm of economic affairs, for there is as much of individualism in their economic philosophy as among the American people. In fact, if cooperation does imply, as our interviews would suggest, that the members of a cooperative must remove their front and lay their cards on the table, this would indeed be so contrary to the Japanese mores of indirectness and reserve that it is very doubtful if they could ever become a cooperative people in this sense. However, where the relationship of the helpers to the helped is the end in itself, as it is in the helpfulness described by Mead, the Japanese must be considered as having a superabundance of help-

---

[14] *The North American Times Year Book, 1936,* p. 9.
[15] Document SX3.
[16] Margaret Mead, *Cooperation and Competition Among Primitive Peoples,* p. 17.

fulness; for, at least from one point of view, the whole complex of Japanese customs is based upon definitions of social relationships in which assignment of traditional responsibilities is carefully worked out for a variety of instances.

In the history of Japanese economic life in Seattle, therefore, we find that primary-group attitudes have been basic in aiding the first establishment of their businesses, and in defending these enterprises from the aggression of their foes. By the same token, these conditions of mutual aid continually acted to enforce and reinforce the solidarity of the community.

But in the failure of the Japanese cooperative we have a suggestion of an underlying dilemma in their economic organization that becomes more and more apparent with each passing year. The failure of the cooperative is essentially to be explained as a failure in the attempt to inject primary-group attitudes into secondary-group relationships. Helpfulness, in other words, has an infinite value in certain types of relationships, but where the same conception is applied without alteration to commercial transactions that transcend friendship relations, the attitude becomes, potentially, a burden to the new situation. It is interesting to note the numerous ways in which this dilemma expresses itself in the trade relations of the Japanese people.

For instance, conceptions of collective obligations have been the crux of the relations between customers and merchants, between retailer and wholesaler, and between retailer and retailer. The remarks of a grocer who once owned a store in the Japanese community but is now trading almost entirely with the white-Americans are enlightening on this point, although they happen to express a resentment against the Japanese conception of helpfulness.

> There are certain difficulties involved in serving Japanese customers. For one thing, the Japanese customer feels that he is the customer, and he thinks the merchant exists to serve his tastes. The Japanese customer will never say "thank you" for anything, but the Americans come around with a feeling that they are happy to be served. The difference lies, I think, in something like this: the Japanese feels that the store continues only because he and many others in that particular district patronize it, and therefore the merchant should be pleased to serve them; but the Americans seem to be glad when they can have a store handy which they did not have before.[17]

Whenever a customer knows of a merchant among his friends who can serve his needs, he is obligated to trade with him, but once the customer enters the store the merchant is expected to show him special favor. Not only the above-mentioned grocer but others of the Japanese merchants who have had to assume the obsequious pose for the benefit of their customers have frequently expressed their resentment.

Recently, however, when the second-generation Japanese, who were neither so conscious of these traditional relations between customers and merchants nor so careful in observing them, started shopping outside the Japanese district since they found a greater variety of goods and prices elsewhere, the Japanese merchants expressed strong disapproval of the youngsters who failed to recognize their obligations as Japanese to trade among the Japanese.

---

[17] Document SX14.

Not only is there this urgency for buying within the Japanese community, but there is further a recognition of *ken* differences and a pressure upon a *ken* member to buy from those of his own *ken*. There is a tendency for this to follow more or less naturally since in-group conceptions among *ken* members become very strong because of the extensive social intercourse that develops on the basis of this single relationship. This comes to mean, of course, that those who belong to the largest *kens,* such as the Hiroshima, Wakayama, Okayama, or Yamaguchi, can expect the widest support from their fellow Japanese, whereas those belonging to the smaller *kens* tend to be left to trade within their own small groups.

The problem that is created is concretely illustrated in the following statement made by an insurance salesman in the community:

> Unless the agent happens to belong to the right *ken* group, it is very difficult for him to sell insurance. For example, I happen to belong to the Kanagawa *ken* which has only a small representation here in Seattle. If I go to the people of the Hiroshima *ken,* or the Okayama *ken,* or any others of such large *ken* group, and if there happens to be an agent from their own group, they will buy from him in preference to me. There is not any personal antagonism against me, but it is simply an expression of their desire to help a member of their *ken* first. I might present any number of arguments showing why they should buy from me, yet they would very likely say vaguely that they will consider it and give me an answer later, and let it go at that. Inevitably, they will buy from a member of their own or related *ken.* Because of these difficulties, and the trouble of attempting to overcome the handicap of my belonging to a minor *ken* group here, I have given up the effort to sell life insurance although I still have a license for selling it.[18]

This statement, in connection with an analysis of another document, presents an interesting hypothesis. In this interview a business man explained that he had gradually dropped his trade with the Japanese because he had found them to be unsatisfactory as customers and had given over 75 per cent of his trade to the white-Americans. Later in the interview he loudly denounced the *ken*-groups, and expressed the opinion that these people ought to be less provincial, just as his own Tokyo-*shi*[19] people were. The hypothesis is suggested that it is the members of the smaller *kens,* having the fewest associations in the Japanese community, who tend first to break away from the community. If this be true, we should find that the members of the Hiroshima, Kumamoto, Yamaguchi, Fukuoka, and others of the large *ken* groups are, on the average, the least assimilated among the Japanese in Seattle.

It is possible to overstress the function of the *ken,* however, and to overlook the stronger bonds which tie one Japanese to another regardless of his other connections. Kinship conceptions, as we have frequently stated before, are the foundation upon which Japanese economic relations seem to operate, and they extend to all levels of society. We may cite one last example of such a relationship in the bonds between the employer and the employee.

There is a tendency among Japanese employers, even today, to make room in their homes for their employees, particularly if they are unmarried. This, of course, was much more common in the earlier periods when unmarried men and

[18] Document SX22.
[19] *Shi,* refers to a metropolitan district. In this statement, therefore, there is a reference to cosmopolitanism with regard to himself.

women were more numerous. The relationship was by no means one-sided, for the obligations resting upon the employers were balanced by corresponding responsibilities on the part of the workers. Today, in the application of this authoritarian attitude by Japanese employers to second-generation employees not trained in this tradition, we find small points of friction arising between the two generations.

Even on levels so far removed as that between contractors for labor and laborers we have the same application of these attitudes. Until two years ago, in the salmon canning industry of Alaska, Oriental cannery workers were employed through Oriental contractors. Working and living conditions in these canneries were, in most instances, extremely poor, though the contractors were making considerable profits even in depression years. The dissatisfaction among the Japanese workers was noticeable, though not overt.

A year ago, however, a drive was made by local labor unions to unionize the cannery workers, which meant doing away with these middle-men and direct bargaining by the labor unions with the industries. While the contractors, mostly Japanese, fought a losing battle, they held the Japanese workers on their side to the last ditch, and the Filipinos, the other major Oriental group among the cannery workers, ultimately usurped control of the labor unions. When the smoke of the battle had cleared, the Japanese laborers who had formerly enjoyed superior status as workers found themselves superseded by the Filipinos.

The failure of the Japanese workers in this instance to break with their employers, though the change was undoubtedly to be for their personal benefit, lay in their inability to break with their traditional conception of collective obligations.

In these economic relationships, therefore, we can observe how both the ethical and kinship conceptions have functioned to tighten the bonds of the community. Among the Japanese there is apparently an ingrown feeling that the relationship between two members of their own nationality is an entirely different thing than the relationship between themselves and other nationalities. In the words of Tönnies, it is the organic will or the natural purpose of the people which is being expressed, that is, their belief that their nation is a product of a single biological heritage and that therefore the people in their relations to one another should act as a family group. These conceptions continue to have applicability because the Japanese hold them sacred, as something that may not be rationally discussed. As a matter of fact, they are continually reinforced in their attitudes toward these conceptions because every economic success which they have is attributed to the providential workings of these primary-group attitudes, whereas every failure is explained in terms of other motivations.

In the projection of these primary-group attitudes into economic areas outside those commonly experienced by the Japanese, however, we have observed incipient signs of disorganization. Certain serious problems which have been created by the credit system as applied within their own community raise doubts about the economic solidarity of their community in the future.

An important white banker in the community, intimate with both American as well as Japanese methods of doing business, replied, when asked concerning the outstanding characteristic of Japanese business:

> The principal one that I have noticed among the Japanese is the weakness in their credit system; their over-extension of credit. You see, the way the Japanese do business among themselves is based entirely on the use of credit, and too small a part of it is on a cash basis. . . . The bad aspect of their credit system is that at the end of the month when it's time to pay up, the Japanese is not likely to pay another Japanese what he owes him, and is likely to let the debt run over into another month or two. Moreover, the Japanese shopkeeper is likely to let the customer run his debts. . . . The result is he finds he can't collect half of these debts. That's the reason why you don't see a single big Japanese business around here. They lose all their profits in their loose credit system.[20]

The inability of the creditor to collect lies in customs which have been transplanted from Japan. If the customer finds that he is unable to pay his bills at the end of the month, he will, as a rule, apologize for his failure to pay at the moment and request an extension of his credit to a later date, to which request the merchant feels compelled to accede. Moreover, from their feudal tradition these Japanese have inherited the attitude that it is indelicate to speak of money matters to one's countryman and, hence they find it difficult to press a question of payment too vigorously.

A person who is in position to know about the financial condition of some of the important Japanese firms in the community says:

> The X Co. is in very bad shape. For example, they have a total account receivable for the last three years of $27,000, and it's difficult to say how much they weren't able to collect prior to that. . . . One of the largest Y firms in the Japanese community has a yearly gross transaction of about $14,000, but their accounts receivable over the last three years total about $6,000. . . . The Japanese business shops have a very good front, but when you get inside, you find out how bad the whole thing is.[21]

An ironical ambiguity exists in the system, however, for while the Japanese are slow to pay when they have a debt with another Japanese, their promptness in paying to the whites has drawn to them a very favorable belief in their business integrity from the latter. Obviously, the Japanese are taking advantage of the obligation which is incumbent upon another Japanese in such trade relations, while in their relations with the larger community, recognizing that they can receive no favoritism, they gladly follow the more rational and impersonal business customs of the whites.

The failure in this instance has been a failure of the Japanese to recognize certain things about their own culture. Extension of credit in the form in which we have found it among the Japanese in Seattle is a rather common and obligatory practice in their native land. As a part of their conception of helpfulness, merchants may not refuse to meet the needs of a family because of the family's lack of money. But the families on their part recognize their duties of repaying their debts, and as a rule do so in the long run. In Japan, under the system of primogeniture, the eldest son inherits not only property but debts as well, and a family

---

[20] Document SX2.
[21] Document SX16.

therefore cannot ever legally declare bankruptcy. In other words, extension of credit is a most satisfactory form of trade relations in a country where families, as well as family property, are relatively stable.

In coming to America these immigrants brought with them the mores for extending credit, but in their early, mobile years created nothing to replace the system of primogeniture which is a necessary complement to the extension of credit. Thus customers could ethically demand and get credit from merchants, but when the critical moment arrived, the merchants had no means of coercing the customers to pay their debts.

The Japanese merchants in the community have learned that these irrationalities in their business cannot long persist without leading to bankruptcy for themselves, and they have attempted to alter these trading customs.[22] Since the customers are, as one man put it, "Very slow to change their ways," and since they will not be coerced within their community, the merchant must either accept the conditions or quit the Japanese trade.

This would suggest that the community is not by any means entirely united, and that while they have a broad background of Japanese traditions in trade relations that tends to enforce community solidarity, these traditions themselves lead into certain dilemmas that the people of the community cannot solve without breaking the very ties that are the foundations of community solidarity.

FAMILY INSTITUTION

It would be easy for an uncritical analyst of the Japanese community to point to family organization as the source of their group solidarity. Unquestionably the efficient controls exercised by the elders of the family would seem to give striking proof of this fact. A closer scrutiny into their social organization reveals, however, that not in the family organization alone, but even more in the relationship between the family and the community do we have the essence of this control. It will be the purpose of this section to elaborate upon this thesis.

In connection with our basic assumption, that immigrant groups always tend to reconstruct their old world institutions, we may profitably study first the Japanese family as it exists in Japan. Recognizing the impossibility of describing their family system in any detail, only four outstanding points shall be mentioned: first, the conception of society as one large family; second, the patriarchal organization of the family, and the consequent male dominance; third, primogeniture and adoption as the system of family inheritance, and the consequent emphasis upon preservation of the family name; and fourth, family customs at birth, marriage, and death.

For the Japanese, the unit of society is not the individual, but the family. Thus, both the Civil and Criminal Code of Japan make the family responsible for the offense of any member within it.[23] This conception of the family as the basic

---

[22] For example, the Japanese merchants have had considerable difficulty in getting their Japanese customers to sign conditional sales contracts for time-payment sales. Document SX1.

[23] De Becker, *Japanese Law,* Vol. III, p. 1.

unit of society is not merely legal fiction, for their whole social life gives explicit expression to it. Even the industrialization of the nation has not changed this condition, and indeed, on the contrary, we find a projection of kinship conceptions into the newly adopted industrial life in Japan. On this point Ayusawa declares:

> Since the adoption of the factory system many Japanese employers have been actuated by the sincere belief that their relations with their employees—however numerous these may be—should be founded on the idea that they all form part of the same family. . . .[24]

On an even wider scale, the conception of Japan as a "nation-wide kinship" seems to be a common expression among the Japanese for the familiar remark that "We Japanese think of our whole nation as one big family because all of the Japanese families are just a branch of the Emperor's noble line,"[25] recurred time and again throughout my interviews.

This idea undoubtedly comes from an extension of the patriarchal family organization developed during feudal periods. Although the power of the male head has gradually diminished, he still has control and supervision over the other members, and they in turn owe him respect and obedience. Authoritarianism thus becomes the cornerstone of the structure, and its influence extends to all who bear the family name. The dominance of the male head as well as of males in general is particularly characterized by contrast with the subordinate position of his spouse, for the good wife in the Japanese sense is one who unquestioningly does the bidding of her husband and raises her children well. The children likewise owe respect and gratitude to their parents for having brought them into the world and reared them, and their obligations are those of repaying with obedience and with a guarantee of security in old age.

Primogeniture, which was a natural development under a feudal patriarchy, survives today in the urban as well as the rural districts of Japan. Property is passed on into the hands of the eldest son of the family, or an adopted son where there are no male heirs present, but while he enjoys these rights, he must also accept the responsibilities of family dependents, family debts, and family problems. Since the family name under a system of primogeniture inevitably becomes associated with the particular property, any shame incurred by a member of the family becomes conspicuously localized in the entire household, and, likewise, any honor to a single member is shared by all his kin. Hence a high premium is placed upon preserving the impeccability of the family name, and this necessity is a primary means of control over the members of a household.

Obviously, in a society where the functions of the family are numerous and of outstanding importance, such events as births, marriages and deaths come to possess great significance. Hence, these occasions of great happiness or of grief are to be shared with all of one's friends, and gift-trading is the symbol of this sympathy. Because of the widespread interest in the community concerning the incidence of these crises, and because these rituals are traditional and overt means

---

[24] I. Ayusawa, *Industrial Conditions and Labour Legislations in Japan, 1926*, p. 3.
[25] Document SX20.

of reinforcing one's friendship sentiments, the observance of these practices becomes extremely important in maintaining one's status among his fellows.

Even from this brief summary of the Japanese family, its structural rigidity by contrast with that of the American family should be apparent. Conceptions of obedience to authority and of maintaining collective responsibilities are of paramount importance within the system, and little room is left for deviations from these norms.

But basic to our problem of community solidarity, we may observe the internal consistency between the attitude of mind taken by the person in the family and that taken by him in the community. To put it in other words, the conception of family in Japan is not a restrictive term as is the case here in America. For the Japanese, not only the group including his immediate blood relatives, but the community and the nation as well, are, in a very real sense, families. It is not so important that they speak of their community or nation as a family; what is really significant is that they act towards it in many ways as if it were a family. Family solidarity is important to community solidarity among the Japanese only in the sense that the two are largely inseparable.

It was with this background that the first immigrants came to America; they came with the deep-seated conviction that the family is the basic institution in society. For them the family was basic in two senses: first, that the individual is subordinate to the family of which he is a member; and second, that primary-group relationships should obtain not only within the kinship group, but also within what in America would be secondary-group relationships. These attitudes were, of course, quite contrary to the family mores of America and, in consequence, this intriguing problem is raised: what happened when the people of a society trained in a collectivistic tradition were grafted upon another society founded essentially on a principle of individualism in the family?

The establishment and growth of family life among the Japanese immigrants to Seattle follow very closely the three fairly distinct periods of community development which I earlier indicated. In the "frontier period" there was little interest in establishing families, but from about 1908 on, the community rather definitely entered into the "settling period," and there was a rapid growth in emphasis upon family life. The Immigration Act of 1924, however, prevented the further entry of marriageable women, and community attention shifted to the rearing of children. Hence, we have named these latter years the "second-generation period." Because of the periodic character in the growth of family life among the Japanese, an historical perspective to our problem will be useful.

Although by 1905 a recognizable Japanese community had formed in Seattle, it had typically frontier characteristics because of its large male population and few families to give it a stabilizing influence. Incomplete sex ratios of the Seattle Japanese during these years give some idea of the sex proportions.

The disproportionate number of males, particularly during the early years, gives some indication of the lack of family life at that time, assuming that a large proportion of the marriageable women would be married if they were available.

TABLE V

POPULATION OF THE JAPANESE IN SEATTLE FOR CERTAIN YEARS
BETWEEN 1900 AND 1920, BY SEX*

Year	Male	Female	Total	Males per Hundred Females
1900	2,739	540	3,279	507
1913	3,246	1,111	4,357	293
1914	3,230	1,318	4,548	245
1917	3,977	1,543	5,520	257
1918	4,323	2,342	6,665	185
1919	4,766	2,718	7,484	175
1920	5,481	3,585	9,066	153

*The North American Times Year Book of 1928, p. 79.

Moreover, prior to 1908 a large number of the women residing in Seattle belonged to a colony of prostitutes within the community, and hence were unmarried; but in that year several of the prostitutes were deported by the United States government, as a result of which most of them fled to the rural areas. At almost the same time a clean-up movement was instituted by a group of young Christians, and they were able to eliminate this undesirable element from the population.

The failure for some time after their arrival of a family-conscious people to establish families can be related, as I have already indicated, to their hope of "getting-rich-quick" and returning to Japan to make their homes, as well as to the fact that many of them were not yet of an age for marriage. As one person put it: "Not one in a thousand came here with the intention of remaining. They all hoped to make enough to go back to Japan."[26] An even stronger point is made by another well-known pioneer of the community:

All of them came over here with the idea that they would stay for about three years, and then go back to Japan to set up their own businesses. Among all whom I know, I can say that not one in a hundred stayed here all the time. The rest of them went back to Japan after a few years, and they came to America again only after they failed in their native land, and found that life in Japan was harder than life over here. But even then, I think in the bottom of their hearts they wanted to go back to Japan to live.[27]

TABLE VI

NUMBER OF JAPANESE FAMILIES IN SEATTLE INTENDING TO
RETURN TO JAPAN IN 1925

Expression of Intention	No. of replies	Per cent
Definitely will not go back	0	0
Would like to return but no prospect at present	258	12.9
Will return to Japan	471	23.6
Undecided	1,271	63.5
TOTAL	2,000	100.0

[26] Document SX8.
[27] Document SX5.

In 1925 the local census made by the Japanese Association included a question upon the intention of families to return to Japan. The 2,000 replies given by the heads of families were classified into the categories indicated in Table VI.[28]

These last data are to be interpreted with much qualification since this census was taken a short time after the passage of the Anti-Alien Land Laws and the Immigration Act of 1924. Feeling ran high within the community, in those years, against the United States government and its policies, and beside the many who may have had to quit their farm land and return to Japan, there were probably those who conscientiously desired to avoid this country as a place to live. Yet, on the other hand, there was an added incentive after the passage of the Immigration Act for the Japanese to remain in this country, for they knew that they would not be permitted to return here should they remain away beyond the life of their passport. That these data are indicative of the general Japanese frame of mind, however, we can probably accept. It is true, they do not show the increased attitude towards settling permanently in the United States which has penetrated a large part of the community in the thirteen years since that census. But even now a prominent minister of this community can complain:

> The weakness of the Japanese community, I would say, lies fundamentally in one fact, namely: the uncertainty of the first generation as to whether they shall spend their lifetime in America, or whether they shall eventually go back to Japan.[29]

The significant point is the extremely slow recession of the feeling that America is just a place to make money, and that Japan is really home. Furthermore, it is only after a presumably temporary home is established in America for the purpose of making enough to return comfortably to Japan, and only after children, who find natural roots in this country, start to come, that the parents resign themselves to a lifetime in America. It is the establishment of the family which makes for the settling down that leads to an involuntary and gradual breaking of ties with Japan.

However, when we analyze the forces tending to keep them within the symbolic structure of Japan, we find that the same family sentiments are the ones strongest in maintaining this orientation. Where one was born, where one's kinsfolk are, where the ancestors are buried and the family shrine stands—all these are for the Japanese the terminal of his deepest sentiments. In the dilemma created by these opposing forces such a factor as economic opportunity becomes a determinant in the choice of his home, and the large number of those undecided in 1925 as to whether or not they shall return to Japan are essentially those who feel the uncertainty of their economic future in America.

This orientation is, of course, important in explaining the absence of family life during the "frontier period," but it serves a more important function in giv-

---

[28] *Seattle Japanese Census of 1925,* taken by the Japanese Association of North America.
[29] Document SX9.

ing us insight into the later life of the community. We see very clearly here how the Japanese immigrant at first made a very obvious distinction between his economic orientation and his social orientation. America was the place to make money, Japan was home. This bifocal orientation of the earlier years seems in the later years, with the establishment of families and relatively permanent business enterprises, to fuse into one. Actually, however, as our data has shown, the Japanese immigrant unconsciously carries the old dual orientation within himself, and what the circumstances of economic necessity and of family growth have forced him to accept, his whole personality, formed within the Japanese social orientation, tends to reject.[30]

This, then, is an important reason for the continuing solidarity of the Japanese community, for the community with its Japanese social life becomes an immediate substitute in the satisfaction of a desire which may not be sated in actuality; thus are the more primitive aspects of the personality structure maintained without conflict. But Japanese community life is nothing except the constellation of Japanese family units functioning in its matrix. For, as we briefly attempted to indicate earlier in this section, occasions of family crises such as births, deaths, and marriages, have relatively little meaning for the Japanese except as they are related to the community life of the people. Among the individualistic type of family such as exists in Western civilization this might not be true to any extent, but within the collectivistic system of the Japanese, family functions are an inseparable part of the community functions.[31]

In the "frontier period," then, there was a lack of family life such as was necessary to give the community its desirable stability. However, the basic social orientation towards Japan and things Japanese, which was to express itself later in a strong sense of social solidarity within the community, had its foundation in this period. It was an inability to break from this earlier orientation that led to the separation of the Japanese community from the larger community surrounding it. Anti-Japanese agitations and other cultural differences served only to heighten this feeling of separateness.

Factors such as the signing of the Gentlemen's Agreement, resulting in a greater selectivity of the emigrants out of Japan; the wider recognition of a necessity to establish homes in the United States if only temporarily; and the increasingly easier adjustment to American life, led to the "settling period" of 1908 to 1924. When the consequent decision to settle in Seattle became more general, the urge to marry and establish homes developed. This urge was further impelled by the traditional Japanese emphasis upon family life, the realization of which was now made possible by their foothold in the economic structure. But the number of women available in Seattle was all too few, and the flow of Japanese women immigrants was far too slow to provide an adequate source of mates for the men. It was necessary, therefore, to devise some means of quickening this flow, and such an instrument was found in the so-called "picture-bride" marriage.

---

[30] It would be interesting to analyze further the conflicts and rationalizations which result from these conditions.
[31] Lafcadio Hearn, *Japan, An Attempt at Interpretation,* pp. 65-118, 443-482.

These were marriages arranged between suitable parties in America and Japan through an exchange of photographs, and agreement by correspondence, after which the girl journeyed to America to be here wedded to the man in the picture. Strange as such a custom may seem to others, a marriage arranged through the exchange of photographs was readily acceptable to the Japanese who had long been accustomed to a system in which marriages were arranged without any direct participation by the young people.

These marriages were arranged, as custom dictated, by "go-betweens," usually relatives or friends who were acquainted with a family having a marriageable daughter. But during this period even the churches and other organizations, such as the *kenjinkai,* assumed this capacity, though it is significant that all attempts to commercialize the position of the "go-between" in the form of marriage bureaus were short-lived.[32] The "go-between's" task was not only to arrange the marriage but also to assume responsibility for the happiness of the couple after their marriage. The married couple, on their part, also incurred an obligation to the "go-between" for the kindnesses received.

It is not to be assumed, of course, that the "picture-bride" marriage was the only means of getting wives for the immigrants. Perhaps as frequently, the men returned to Japan themselves to bring back their wives. In some instances, sight-seeing tours *(kankodan),* which were formed ostensibly for young men desiring to tour Japan, were actually for the purpose of finding wives. Whatever the manner of choosing the future wife, however, the marriages were usually arranged. In the large majority of cases wives were chosen from the same *ken* as that from which the husband came.[33]

In these efforts to establish families, the basic point to be noted is the significant functioning of the traditional Japanese community in bringing about these marriages. The inability of the marriage agencies to commercialize the function of the "go-between" is an eloquent expression of the sacredness of their community traditions. The net effect of participation by friends, churches, and other organizations in bringing to consummation the happy meeting of husband and wife was undoubtedly to strengthen the bonds of intra-community relationships.

The world into which these provincial young Japanese women came was strange and new. Most of them had been raised strictly in accordance with the traditional Japanese notion of women's inferior status in society, so each possessed the virtues of fatalistic acceptance in the face of hardship, of industry, and of thorough training in Japanese proprieties. But they were ill-prepared to adapt themselves to a mechanistic, individualistic, Western society. It was common practice to rush the women dressed in kimonos directly from the pier where they landed to a hotel, there to have a dressmaker and shoe-salesman measure them for an American-style outfit. Thus her first act upon landing here was to lose the folkway closest to her from childhood, the wearing of a kimono and all its accessories.

---

[32] Document SX8.

[33] In a small sample of twenty-nine families, 76 per cent of the husbands and wives were from the same *ken.* See also Lafcadio Hearn, *op. cit.,* pp. 106-107.

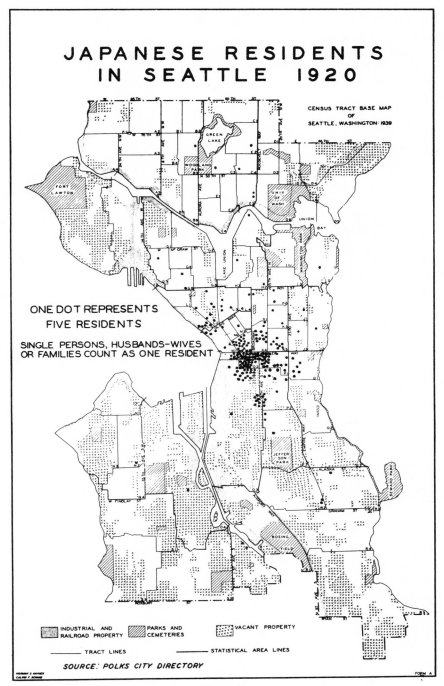

Figure I

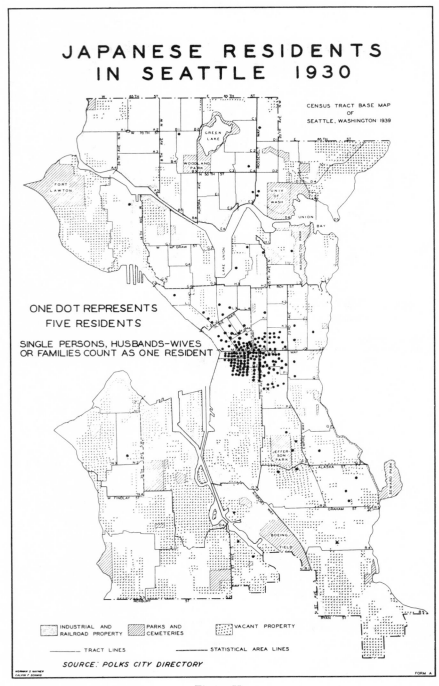

Figure II

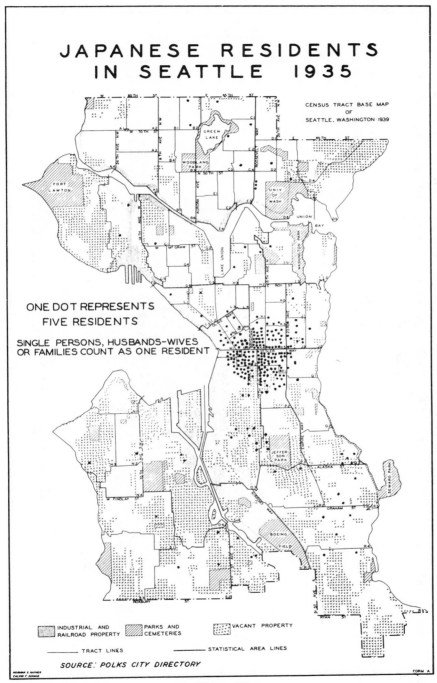

Figure III

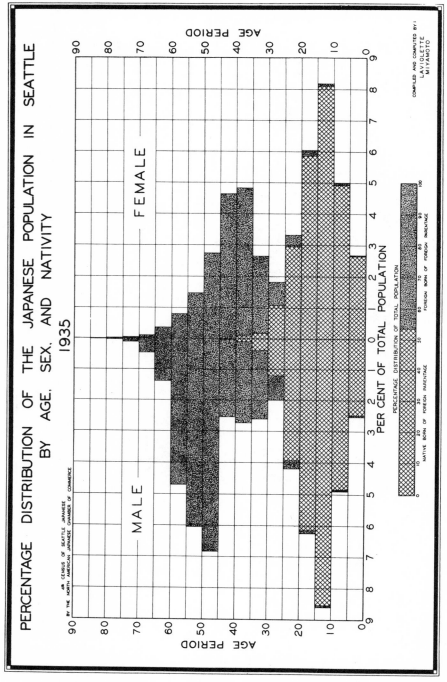

Figure IV

The hotels and rooming-houses around Main and Jackson streets flourished in those days, for it was in these places that the newly married couples tended to establish their first homes. Private dwellings were a comparatively unknown thing as the statement of an old-time resident indicates:

> In 1900 there were only three families with what might be called private homes, and all of the rest lived in rooming-houses or in hotels. . . . Even as late as 1910 people still lived in rooming-houses, and the back-rooms of shops. Of course, there weren't so many of the latter at that time. They didn't even have apartment rooms in any great numbers. . . . During the years from 1910 to about 1918, many of the people leased large homes and rented several of their rooms to other families or to single men.[34]

Just what the effect was of living in this type of home is difficult to say. Very probably it retarded the immigrants in gaining a true conception of normal American home life, for into their narrow hotel and rooming-house dwellings, they brought a strange admixture of Japanese and American atmosphere. We can, however, more definitely say that this crowding into urban rooming-houses and hotel rooms did not make for a greater anonymity as has been so commonly noted of American urban life. With the tradition of extending primary-group relationships beyond the bounds of family life deeply instilled in them, the direct effect was to bring the nigh-dwellers very close together. In the Japan of that time, and even today in the non-metropolitan areas, the neighborhood relationships tend to be highly intimate.

> The neighborhood was very important in Japan. Everybody who lived on a given block tended to form a social unit. For example, in Japan we have things very similar to the spring-cleaning here in America. On those occasions the neighbors all used to get together to help each other out.[35]

Hence, in the first few bewildering months after arrival, there were always the friends and neighbors to guide the newcomers in adjusting themselves to their new environment. Even the shopkeepers seldom acted as mere functionaries, but they were rather countrymen who could be called upon to aid in the adjustment process. One grocer makes this remark about the trade of that time:

> In the old days there were times when I frequently used to furnish the whole kitchen requirements for the women, from the pots and pans down to the smallest cooking utensils.[36]

Throughout this period of family establishment, therefore, we can observe how conceptions of collective responsibility and community *esprit de corps* operated to ease the adjustment to an immigrant family life. It was undoubtedly in just such circumstances as these that their traditions of helpfulness functioned at their best. Even today the memory of the days of mutual aid are frequently recalled in conversations, and the solidarity of the people is thus reinforced.

This period of family establishment and primary adjustments was abruptly ended by the passage of the Immigration Act in 1924. While there still were undoubtedly many lingering desires among the people of the community to return to

---

[34] Document SX10.
[35] Document SX10.
[36] Document SX14.

Japan, a large part of the population had reconciled themselves to life in this country, and some had definitely decided to settle. With the problems of the first-generation adjustment rapidly receding, therefore, the community concern shifted its focus to the problems of bringing up children.

Living as most of these families did in a crowded transition area, the children had only the busy streets and the vacant lots to play in. Moreover, they were in the center of Seattle's worst criminal zone, the notorious "Profanity Hill" of this city. The parents themselves were in most cases busy during the day earning the rather limited incomes possible from their small shops, and they had little time to give to their children. The chief comfort which they had was in the thought that the family would be together in the evenings.

With regard to the youngest children, the problem was solved in part by kindergartens started in various missions and churches. These were institutions in which the parents placed great trust, both as places for Americanization and as places where the children would gain a correct moral training. For the older children, there were the daily public schools and the late afternoon Japanese Language School between the two of which the entire day was, as a rule, largely taken up. While these institutions were essentially for learning and only incidentally for child care, it is significant that they functioned very efficiently for the latter purpose. Furthermore, they were integral to the community, not outside it. Through them the community was able both to impress the solidarity of the people upon the children, as well as to gain unity from the common participation.

To understand fully the Japanese family controls exercised upon its members, however, we should perhaps start at the core of the family system and work outwards, for the relationship of individuals and groups to each other, their relatives, their community, and their nation, can be represented as a series of ever-widening concentric circles of relationships throughout which a pattern of collective responsibility is interwoven. It is this which gives a consistency and unity between the family and the community, and minimizes the distinctions between them. We may start by observing the male head as the dominant center of the family.

The omnipotence of the male head, it is true, is not so marked in this community as it was in Japan, for the women enjoy relatively greater freedom here, but in such significant phases of married life as the forming of decisions on important matters and in the final authority of control, the dominance of the male head remains largely unabated. The persistence of these standards is largely dependent upon the fact that the women themselves respond to a subordinate role.

> Of course, I feel sometimes that he (the husband) is a little too hard on the children, and I feel that it is better to treat them more as companions than as children to be dominated, but, you know, it isn't possible for the wife to tell the husband how he should act, so I only try to soften what he says.[87]

> It seems to me that the American husband is very much henpecked, isn't he?[88]

One might assume that upon being released from the extreme rigidity of the Japanese social system, the Japanese women would take advantage of their new

---

[87] Document SX13.
[88] Document SX7.

freedom to seek out new worlds of experience, and to attempt to equalize their differential status. However, trained as they were to subordination and to a philosophy of fatalism, there was nothing in their psychology, and very little in their experience in America, to create shifts in attitudes. In fact, the women of the community were themselves the most critical of those among them who deviated from the norm and they, in consequence, tended to formulate and set the standards by which they limited their own behavior. The stereotypes held by Japanese women of the American women are those of the latter being served breakfast in bed by their husbands, of their spending their days in a whirl of social affairs without giving proper attention to their children, of husband-wife relationships as being of the "Maggie-Jiggs" cartoon variety; and the highly individualized white women are rather objects of criticism than of envy. Thus, where the father is the chief symbol of status and of the duties and privileges which are a part of his heritage, the mother is the mouthpiece which constantly reinforces this.[39]

The male head also assumes dominance over the children, and the mother as a representative of the father reflects a certain amount of this authority. By comparison with white-American children, the activities of Japanese children are generally more regulated by their parents. In extreme instances, though these are infrequent, this authority extends itself into a practical control over every important action of the children. The result is either docility on the part of the growing boy or girl to parental regulation, or an underlying irritation from it that threatens to break out in overt rebellion and necessitates a constant readjustment of relationships between them.

The parents, on their part, rationalize this authoritarianism on an ethical basis, for the Japanese parents conceive their chief duty to be a concern over the welfare of their children. The apparent lack of regulation by American parents of their children's lives is interpreted by the Japanese as being an insufficient concern about the children's welfare. A minister explained the differences of attitude in this manner:

> In the American family a youngster, after he reaches a certain age, is responsible only to himself. A father can cay: "Well, I taught my son to do sc-and-so. If he doesn't do as I instructed, I can't help it now." But with a Japanese father it is different. He says: "I taught my son in such-and-such a way, and now he is old enough to know what is right himself. Yet he is irresponsible and cannot take care of himself. I must set him right; I wonder what I must do to make him understand."[40]

The strength of this authority lies not alone in the dominant role assumed by the parents, but even more in the reinforcement given by the community to this parental status. Upon every public occasion at which parents and children are gathered, the tendency is to remind the young of the virtues of obedience. Every

---

[39] The subordination of the Japanese women may be an outstanding force retarding Japanese assimilation. One Japanese observes with keen insight: "I'll tell you why the Japanese people don't get Americanized more rapidly. It's because the Japanese women don't get out more and mix with the Americans. In America the social life is built up largely around the women, and it's the women who say: 'Well, Daddy, there's a party going on tonight, and we're going out.' But the Japanese women never try to get out and mix."

[40] Document SX9.

visitor in the home is careful to make observations concerning the quietness of the children, or of their obedience, and the parents are prone to discuss the matter with hidden pride. In the Japanese schools, the Japanese churches, and in any organizations where the older generation have a part, the subject of obedience and of filial piety is frequently brought to the forefront. It is thus through constant discussion and agreement over these basic ideals that their importance becomes impressed upon the children, and because of the total agreement in the community about these primary ideals, no propaganda gets a more effective reiteration.

Since there is this agreement in the community about these ethical principles, and since status in the community depends upon the observance of these basic ideals, another means of parental control exists in an appeal to the children's sense of respect for the family name. Every caution and every reprimand, therefore, is accompanied by a reminder of the necessity for preserving the status of the name, and of attempting to raise it if possible. What others will think of one's behavior looms large in the minds of the Japanese and controls their behavior extensively. This pressure, undoubtedly, is of basic importance in explaining the strong Japanese interest in keeping up a front and preserving "face." Family control, therefore, is not simply parental control, but community control as well. It is the family in relation to the community that becomes the decisive force in regulating the behavior of individuals within the group. The fact that there is wide participation in the local community makes possible this form of control.

It is where the unified relationship between the family and the community breaks down that we observe signs of disorganization setting in. For instance, while the parents hold the relation between themselves and their children to be sacred no equal feeling is evidenced by their American-born children, educated in another community. The Japanese parents cannot understand why the American-born children are not as obedient and respectful towards their elders as are the children of Japan; they are shocked at having their children ask to be paid for doing menial tasks about the home. These are the differences which bring most pointedly into consciousness for the older generation the social distance which actually separates the two generations, and this is the problem in the parent-child relationship which most deeply concerns the parents today. The concern which the parents feel is made apparent by the frequency with which they discuss the matter with their children. An interesting instance of this reminding process occurred at a wedding of a young American-born couple when one of the functionaries, being called upon to speak, took the occasion to instruct the bride and the groom in their responsibilities toward their parents after they set up their own family.[41]

The fact that such an occasion should have been taken to reinforce the conceptions of filial piety is very likely an indication of the breakdown of the mores in the younger people. The older members of the community view with sadness the uncertainty of their condition. As one person put it:

---

[41] Document SX24.

Here in America, the children, as soon as they grow up, feel that they can leave their parents; that the parents can take care of themselves. The duty of the parents they know has been to bring up their children properly, but they do not understand the principle of reciprocating that duty. In Japan every old person is cared for by his children; they can have a life of leisure when the children have become old enough to make a living themselves. That is why I often wish that I could go back to Japan and live.[42]

An interesting expression of the uncertainty felt by the older Japanese of the community lies in the amount of life insurance policies which have been taken out by them. Having lost the security of a livelihood provided by their children in their old age, they have sought the more rationalized American method of preparing for their declining years. One Japanese insurance agent who has been selling policies for the last twenty-five years declared:

Unlike the American community, everybody, or at least almost everybody (referring only to the family heads), in the Japanese community has taken out some kind of a life policy. The reason for this lies in the fact that while in Japan these same people would have had security in simply belonging to a certain family group. Here the family system has broken down and there is none to turn to in case of the death of the bread winner. . . . Thus, while there was at first a general disinterestedness in insurance policies, and as a matter of fact, there existed even an aversion for the reason that they couldn't understand the policies and had some fears of entering into contracts which they couldn't readily interpret, about the latter part of the war period, we had an unusual boom in the insurance business.[43]

It is not that the children are entirely unconcerned about the welfare of their parents. In fact, the American-born Japanese are, in many instances, deeply conscious of their obligations towards their parents, but when conflicting desires arise, there is not the certainty about what they will do that is true of a young person in Japan. It is noteworthy, however, that with increased maturity and with the attainment of some economic stability, the second generation are beginning to give evidence of the kind of family responsibility for which the older generation have been asking.[44] In this the second generation who most ideally follow the Japanese tradition set the pace, and the rest find it necessary to follow. The elders of the community bring pressure upon the unconforming by idealizing and using as exemplars those most closely adhering to the accepted Japanese behavior pattern.

The circle of family activities does not stop within the family proper, but a tendency towards widening these circles to include the largest group possible constantly operates. Occasions of births, marriages, and deaths are particularly important in this respect, for the Japanese have inherited certain customary ways of expanding the extent of collective sympathies at these times of crises. Upon occasions of births, for example, not only are congratulations in order, but gift-exchanges between the parents and friends take place. This stands in contrast to the American custom because of the extensiveness of gift-exchanging. Marriages likewise call for the recognition of such reciprocal obligations. To the necessity of having various functionaries intervene at the times of marriage must be added

[42] Document SX8.
[43] Document SX22.
[44] Forrest LaViolette, *Types of Adjustment Among Second-Generation Japanese* (unpublished doctor's thesis, University of Chicago, Chicago. In preparation).

the necessity for sharing the happiness of the occasion with all the family friends. One of the chief problems faced by young Japanese couples getting married today is the problem of properly acknowledging all the obligations to family friends, and their exceptionally large weddings, out of all proportion to their incomes, are a result of the necessity for recognizing these various obligations.

No occasion, however, calls for a greater extension of primary-group sentiments outside the actual limits of the family than the death of a family member. The differences from the American funeral customs consist largely in the more voluminous exchanges of sympathy in the Japanese community. Added to this, however, is the traditional Japanese custom of giving *koden* (money gifts at times of death) to aid in the payment of funeral expenses, and when the average *koden* amounts to anywhere from one dollar to twenty or more dollars per family, the accumulation of two or three hundred dollars in gifts at a funeral is not an unusual occurrence.

Such concrete interchanges of sympathy as these come to have extreme significance in drawing the community together. It is not alone the gift-exchanging with its symbolism of sympathy which is effective in bringing about community solidarity, but it is the recognition of obligations incurred that strengthens the group bonds. Not only does the mourning family receive these gifts, but frequently they reciprocate with an elaborate reception following the funeral; and on later occasions when other people in the community die, the family must remember their earlier obligations. Nor does the commemoration of the dead end with the funeral, but the gathering of close friends occurs every seventh day through the forty-ninth, and among the more strict Japanese families, even more frequently than that.

It is impossible in this limited space to show all the ramifications in family and community relationships that bring the group together, but in our discussion we have attempted to show that social solidarity is based not alone on the authoritarianism of their family system, but rather upon the inseparable interdependence of the community and the family. This interdependence was, we pointed out, historically a result of the immigrant's early orientation backward towards Japan, an orientation that persists among many even to this day. Faced as they are in that direction the immigrant personalities and families cannot fit themselves into an American community, so they prefer the life of their own ghetto. In the Japanese tendency to look upon the community as a primary group we have a still more dynamic solidifying factor, for through this tradition the people are able to call upon the community to aid in establishing families, in bringing up and controlling the young, and in exchanging collective sympathy on occasions of life crises. Finally, no disorganization shows in such a community because the personality as it functions and develops within the family is entirely consistent with the personality that must live actively within the community. It is difficult to say of such an organization that the community or the family is the chief solidifying factor, for in essence the two flow imperceptibly into each other, and solidarity exists primarily in the bond between the two.

RELIGIOUS INSTITUTIONS

In discussing the influence of religious institutions upon social solidarity, we may not, as in our treatments of the economic and family organization, assume the institutions to be homogeneous for the whole community. In fact, in Christianity and Buddhism, the two dominating religions, we have churches that are moving in two different directions. The basis of these differences lies in certain fundamental dissimilarities in their theology, and for people of Western civilization essentially influenced by Christianity, Buddhism must seem strange and difficult to appreciate.

Without attempting to discuss in detail the variant theologies of each religion, it is sufficient for our purpose to call attention to a few striking contrasts in their points of view. DeBenneville puts it well when he says:

> Christianity, no matter how much it preaches humility, is essentially a militant religion. . . . It is this practical application which has given it such force among the Aryan peoples of Europe, to whom dreamy abstractions as to a dim and uncertain future life would appeal but little. . . . It teaches him that as man living in this world he cannot avoid contact with sin, and hence he must combat sin wherever he finds it. . . . Buddhism has the genuine spirit of monasticism. . . . Avoidance of the world and hence avoidance of sin. Merit is to be obtained by combating sin but can equally be obtained by avoiding temptation. Where Christianity preaches war against sin as the only practical means of salvation, Buddhism, in the contrary, preaches resignation, the uselessness of struggle for this world which is merely phenomenal.[45]

These differences in their basic structure lead to certain differences of attitudes, for where the Buddhist learns to accept his fate *(akirameru)* with regards to his earthly life, the Christian aggressively tries to make over his destiny. Whereas the Buddhist tends to seek out the "middle path," the Christian tries to seek out an extreme. The Buddhist attempts to adjust to his world, or tends to accept it as it is, while the Christian struggles to make over his world. These distinctions serve to raise some very interesting problems when we inquire into the religious institutions of the Japanese in Seattle.

The first question is raised when we compare the memberships of the Christian churches with those of the Buddhist and Shinto churches. The numbers in 1936 were as follows:[46]

TABLE VII

MEMBERSHIP IN JAPANESE CHURCHES IN SEATTLE, 1936

Religion	No. of Members
Christian	1,200
Shinshu Buddhist	650
Nichiren Buddhist	150
Shinto	120
Tenrikyo	60

---

[45] James S. DeBenneville, *More Japonico,* pp. 84-85.
[46] Document SX9.

In interpreting these figures we must recognize that while the Christian church figures are for actual members, the Buddhists, who have not been accustomed to congregational meetings in Japan, count adherents also, as for instance in the case of the Shinshu sect where the actual membership is 250 rather than 650.

The important fact is that the membership of the Japanese Christian churches in Seattle far outnumbers those of the native Japanese religions, and this stands in striking contrast to the relative slowness of Christianity to gain acceptance in Japan.[47] It is necessary, therefore, to inquire what it was that gave Christianity its dominant position among the Japanese in Seattle. To understand the process by which the Japanese became converted to their new religion, we must again view the historical growth of the community.

As we earlier indicated, in the "frontier period" the community was made up largely of unmarried men eager to make their stake and then return to Japan to set up their own businesses. They were, of course, mostly men with relatively little status in the community, but by the same token they were also men who had relatively few social contacts. It was among these people that the American Christian missionaries began to do their work and to find a very fertile soil for propagating their religious ideas.

The principal interest of the Japanese immigrants was, of course, to make a quick "clean-up" in America and then return to Japan. In accomplishing this purpose the Christian churches served extremely important functions. The first necessity was that of getting jobs, and in this the church served as an employment agency, especially sending out a large number of house-boys, known in those days as "mission-boys."[48] There was, too, the immediate necessity of becoming acquainted with the American ways of behavior, speaking, and understanding, and in consequence the churches became centers in which the young immigrants, ambitious to learn the language and thus to rise in the American economic scale, crowded in with hope of improving themselves.

The significance of this social welfare work launched by the Christian missions lies in the fact that by this work they were playing directly upon the most deeply laid collectivistic sentiments of the Japanese people, and it is little wonder that these immigrants formed favorable attitudes toward Christianity. Nothing in Japan is more sacred than the helpfulness of one member of society towards another, and the Christian missionaries with their practice of benevolent aid to the young immigrants arriving on these shores must have endeared themselves to these people. Many, too, were Christians before they reached these shores, for it was those first Christians of the Meiji era who were most struck by the spirit of adventuring across the seas, influenced as they had been by the tales of wonder told them by the early Christian missionaries.

By strange contrast, the Buddhist Church was grievously barren of such organizational work, for it was not a part of Buddhist traditions, and it may even

---

[47] *Japan Year Book 1935*, p. 823.
[48] Document SX4.

have been that these immigrants compared the native Buddhist church unfavourably in the light of their failure to provide a similar organization. In Japan there had never been any need for the American type of mission church since these functions were more than adequately provided for in their family system. Thus, by a remarkable displacement, the Christian churches came to fit, here in America, much more into the traditional mores of the Japanese people than did their native religious institutions, and Christianity was given a strong impetus from the first towards gaining a large following. To the Japanese with their deep sense of moral obligation of one man to another, and of a social organization to its members, the principles of the Christian churches and their missionary efforts must have seemed highly commendable.

There were other disadvantages faced by Buddhism in attempting to gain ascendancy. For one thing, Buddhism is in large part a religion of the home, but in these early frontier years there were no Japanese homes to speak of, and the very mobility of the people must have greatly weakened their traditions of ancestor worship. Perhaps a persistence of this instability might have broken down to a degree their traditional piety towards Buddhism. Furthermore, Buddhism is essentially Oriental in its institutional practices and offers nothing of Western culture, but many of the immigrants of that day were primarily interested in learning about America. What advantages Buddhism did have lay in the fact that it constantly tended to keep alive the memories of the Japanese people about their native land, and it is certainly no accident that the Buddhist Church was first in promoting a Japanese language school for the children of the immigrants.

With a shift to the "Settling period" the chief functions of the church became that of a marriage bureau and an agency for aiding in the establishment of families. On occasion the church even functioned as "go-between" for the unmarried men seeking wives in Japan, while with the large numbers of "picture-bride" marriages taking place in this country the churches became extremely busy institutions. With respect to performing marriage ceremonies, the Christian churches again had certain advantages, in that with their relatively simple forms, the ceremony itself was facilitated. It was natural, moreover, for the Christian ceremony to be widely used since the Japanese custom of marriage before the family shrine was not possible for the immigrants far removed from their native land.

With the births of children, however, the importance of the Buddhist churches increased, for the families practicing the traditional Japanese birth rites found it convenient to call the Buddhist priest. Moreover, the more religious Buddhist parents found it desirable to send their children to the Buddhist Sunday schools where they might be instructed in the traditional Buddhist practices, particularly since the American educational system provided no place whatsoever for any religious or ethical instruction.

There were again, however, certain advantages to be had from the Christian missions that were not presented in the Buddhist institutions. Since many of the parents worked during the day, they faced the problem of providing care for their children during those hours. The Christian churches provided the means of meeting this problem with their kindergartens under the instruction of white teachers and particularly in the earlier years there were relatively few children who did not spend their first schooling in either the Methodist or the baptist kindergartens. Nor were the Americanizing functions of the Christian kindergartens of any little importance, for coming as the children did from homes that were almost entirely Japanese in their essential features, the transition from Japanese home life to an American public grammar school was made easier through the functioning of the kindergartens.

Mission schools also provided a degree of informality and hence of intimacy which in many cases, enabled parents to become acquainted with the white teachers of their children, and in a sense, the church kindergartens came to serve as an indirect source of learning for the Japanese mothers. A more direct and significant influence, however, was the manner in which the parents came to be drawn in as members of the churches in consequence of their children's attendance at the Christian kindergartens. The major portion of the time in these missions was given over to secular instruction, but there was a certain amount of religious instruction as well, and the children tended to be drawn into the Sunday schools. Thus the parents became acquainted with the traditions of the Christian Church.

Through this second period we find the churches enjoying a vigorous growth, in the first place because they played an important part in the establishment of families, and more significantly because of parental interest in giving to their children a proper moral training. The Japanese emphasis upon ethical training was undoubtedly of great importance in stimulating the growth of the churches, for lacking this instruction in the public schools, the parents felt strongly the necessity of meeting this need in other institutions. The following expresses the feelings of many Japanese parents:

> I told my children that it didn't matter whether they went to a Christian church or a Buddhist church, but that they should go to some kind of a church. Since their friends were going to the Methodist Church, they went there, but after I joined the Congregational Church, I transferred them to the latter.[49]

Especially since the passage of the Immigration Act has the focus of religious attention been turned even more to the second generation, and the churches voice the necessity of giving greater weight to their religious and moral training. One pastor declares:

> In any case, our whole program at the present is centered upon the work among the second-generation. The first-generation are passing out, and there is little more work to be done among them, except in so far as good Christian parents inevitably have better Christian children. For that reason we are trying to bring more and more of the first-generation into the churches.[50]

In the meantime, however, the older generation have built up a large system of religious organizations, and participation within these organizations has strengthened the feeling of communal solidarity. Frequent meetings, aside from the regular Sunday ones, are necessary for various occasions and businesses.

---

[49] Document SX13.
[50] Document SX4.

There are the problems of financing which need to be met by donations and contributions. There are the numerous home meetings held in turn among the different families of a church in as widely divergent parts of the city as Green Lake and South Park. And for each birth, marriage, and death, and for every departure and return to and from Japan or other points, there again is an occasion for a round of activities that bring the group together. Throughout all of this is intertwined the system of courtesies that are inevitably a part of the meetings of a Japanese group, and that serve to constantly reinforce the feelings of group obligations.

For the women of the community, the church has made possible an extension of their social activities which they could not otherwise have developed, for in Japanese tradition women's place has been in the home, and there have been no organizational means of enlargening their social world. Since every increase of social contacts in the Japanese community means added occasions for the reinforcement of Japanese sentiments, this expansion of the women's world has tended to increase the social solidarity of the community. Moreover, the numerous bazaars and social affairs which are now a significant part of Japanese church work are sponsored in the main by the women, and these contacts have made for increased acquaintanceship and financial mutual aid such as they were not able to enjoy before.

It is not alone because the Japanese people participate intensely within their church structure that group solidarity is strengthened; even more is it because a complex overlapping of organizational participation exists. For example, many of the prominent leaders in the Japanese Association are also men who are leaders in their respective churches, and thus there is a tendency to bridge the differences between organizations by common personal relationships.

In a long perspective, the social solidarity of the community seems to be affected differently by the Buddhist Church than by the Christian, as we mentioned earlier in this section. It is perhaps unwise to generalize with regard to the influence of the Christian or Buddhist religions on personality, but as Christianity is indigenous to a culture that is mobile, individualistic, and inclined to action, it seems to impress upon its church members these same characteristics; whereas Buddhism which is indigenous to a relatively immobile, collectivist, and nonactive culture seems likewise to mold its adherents along lines in accord with its tradition.

It would seem, then, that a person who feels social ambitions transcending anything a fatalistic Buddhist philosophy would approve might possibly turn to Christianity, for where the Buddhist would resign himself to fate, a person of Christian faith would feel that he should change the world rather than accept it as it is. Such a statement as the following would lead one to think that this tendency is present:

> In Japan I was a Buddhist of deep faith. . . . After coming to America, how-
> ever, I changed to Christianity because I felt that there was something in it which
> Buddhism did not have. In Buddhism they talk a great deal about cause and effect,
> and about destiny, but they have nothing in it which says anything about what one
> can do himself to change himself or his world. In Christianity, however, we learn
> that it is possible to alter the way of life and one's destiny by one's own acts. This
> is the thing which I have come to feel is important, and that is the reason I have
> given up my Buddhism and taken up Christianity.[51]

From this standpoint, the Christian churches, with their emphasis upon individual worth, should tend to draw the Japanese away from their traditional
mores of collectivism, and reduce their respect for such conceptions as collective
obligations. This is quite evident in the greater emphasis which Buddhism inevitably places upon the basic ideas of ancestor worship, and in its closer adherence
to the traditional customs of Japan, particularly the rituals in connection with life
crises.

The conclusion to which one is led from such considerations is that Christianity, which in the earlier stages was instrumental in bringing about a type of
community solidarity based upon organizational activities, is possibly in the later
stages, through its tendency to break down the conceptions of collective responsibility, tending to destroy Japanese community solidarity. That this will take
place shortly is unlikely, but the long-time effect, it would seem, might possibly
be in that direction. Buddhism, on the contrary, by its very nature orients the
members of its congregation towards Japan. For instance, a Buddhist priest declared that his English was poor because he rarely had occasion to use it in his
church work, which is something that would be impossible in a Christian church.
And by this orientation Buddhism turns the Japanese community inward, and
stresses the differences between it and the American community. One may well
question whether, in recent years with an increasing number of first-generation
Japanese reaching a period in life when the rites to the dead take on a more personal meaning, the Buddhist faith may not have gained a new importance which
it did not possess during these men's more vigorous years.

Educational Institutions

Perhaps no better understanding of the relationship betwen education and
Japanese community solidarity can be had than by quoting a most lucid statement bearing upon this point made by Lafcadio Hearn. He declares:

> The aim of Western education is the cultivation of individual ability and per-
> sonal character—the creation of an independent and forceful being.
> Now Japanese education has always been conducted, mostly upon the reverse
> plan. Its object never has been to train the individual for independent action, but to
> train him for cooperative action—to fit him to occupy an exact place in the mechan-
> ism of a rigid society.[52]

In Japanese educational tradition the individual is trained for the task of fit-
ting into a particular status in society; he is trained so that he may better recognize the obligations incumbent upon a member of society, and better utilize the

---

[51] Document SX13.
[52] Lafcadio Hearn, *Japan, An Interpretation,* p. 460.

privileges which are his lot. To put it another way, he is trained deeply in an appreciation of traditional social values, while the development of individual values is minimized. The net effect of this is a strengthening of the group consensus, and a levelling out of all individual differences that may tend to destroy the strength of these bonds.

In a society where group ideals are clearly defined by tradition, the marks of an educated man are stereotyped, and popular opinion places an extraordinary valuation upon his accomplishments. Furthermore, in Japan where ethical ideals are as important as the pecuniary ones principally idealized here in America, formal school training has a far greater significance in determining the superior status of an individual. In consequence, education symbolizes a common goal of endeavor for the members of a community, and the focalized participation in the institution draws the members of the group together.

By the same token, since education has an ethical association, a certain sacredness surrounds the institution. Every Japanese community feels a strong duty about educating its young, and this projects itself down into a deep concern on the part of the parents over the training of their children. Since the parents' discharge of this duty is measurable only in terms of their children's performance, a duty likewise accrues on the part of the children to strive to their utmost in their school work, and thus pay their filial obligations.

It is perhaps significant that for the Japanese in Seattle this interest in schooling had no basis in the amount of education which the immigrants themselves had in Japan. Even a rough estimation as to the amount of their schooling gives clear evidence of the fact that they averaged considerably less than graduation from middle-school (corresponds roughly to our high school[53]). Data on the illiteracy of the Japanese in Seattle over twenty-one years of age, almost all of whom would be immigrants, shows a rate of 12.2 per cent in 1930.[54] Most of these immigrants failed to get more education because of lack of opportunity, for when we observe the vigor of the educational interest among the Japanese in Seattle today, we can assume that education was in the mores of the people and that it only awaited an opportune moment for its pursuance. There is, as a matter of fact, strong evidence that a great deal of the educational aggressiveness among the Japanese here has come about because they feel so keenly their early lack of educational opportunities.

As evidence on this point, we may cite the manner in which English language schools flourished from the early days of the community. A pioneer in the community recalls that:

---

[53] A small sample of twenty-seven university students gave the amount of their fathers' education as:

More than high school	5
High school graduate	8
Grammar school graduate	12
Less than grammar school graduate	2

[54] U. S. Census, 1930, Vol. II, Table 23, p. 1302. The rate seems extremely high, and the way in which illiteracy was determined might be questioned.

> The English classes have always been popular among the Japanese, and they go back as far as 1898 .... the mission night schools have attracted most of these men who were still fairly young and ambitious and quite interested in learning to understand English.[55]

This strong interest in English schools is surprising since most of these Japanese had no definite intention of remaining more than a few years in America. Moreover, the learning of English was a difficult task for them because it differs so widely from their native tongue. But among other factors, the ambition of these immigrants is undoubtedly of basic importance in explaining such widespread effort at learning, for by the learning of English they hoped to better their economic standing and thus improve their status.[56] It is of course true that ambition is not peculiar to the Japanese people alone, but it possesses among them a peculiarly rigid character that gives it an appearance of vigor. The Japanese, unlike the Americans, are not inclined to seek new ways of attaining a particular ambition, but have certain prescribed patterns through which they must toil.

This recalls an interesting point with respect to their educational institutions already suggseted in the quotation from Hearn, namely, the great dependence which the Japanese tend to lay upon formal education as a means of attaining knowledge, and the relatively small place they give to pragmatic methods as a means of broadening their background. The very lack of proficiency indicated by the Japanese in their usage of English, despite the fact that they attempted to study it, is the result of their effort to gain a knowledge of the language from books rather than by daily practice in conversation. To practice the language before others and to make errors during this training does too much violence to the Japanese feelings of reserve and "front," and thus the very desire for status which gives them interest in studying the language becomes, at the same time, a hindrance to the natural progress of the learning process. If the Japanese could place himself in an American frame of mind, he no doubt could free himself from these inhibitions, but his inability to readjust himself in this regard prevents his assimilation, and tends to perpetuate the solidarity of the community.

In a modified way these are the same values in education which have been taken over by the second generation, and the striking scholastic record which they have made is largely to be explained in terms of the community background out of which they have come.

Considering the educational institutions of the Japanese community from a historical point of view, we may note certain periodic shifts in the educational interests of the community from one type of school to another, the periods changing with the rise of the age level among the second generation. (See Figure IV.) It is difficult to delineate with exactness the various periods, but public grammar schools were the focus of community attention in the few years before and after the building of the Bailey Gatzert School in 1921. There were years around 1915 and 1920 when almost all of the Japanese children in the community started their schooling at the old Main Street School located at Sixth Avenue and Main Street

---

[55] Document SX8.
[56] Document SX20.

in the center of the Japanese business district, but with the expansion of the Japanese grammar school population the erection of the Bailey Gatzert School became necessary. A certain part of the school population moved out into the Central, Pacific, and Washington school districts immediately surrounding the Japanese community.

In this period when interest was chiefly in the grammar schools the significant feature was the close relationship between the community and the schools, reflected in the direct association between the parents and the teachers. Due to the ecological segregation of the Japanese children mainly into two or three school districts,[57] the parents were able to feel that the schools were a part of the Japanese community. They thus had the courage to participate directly in them. It is not alone the parents' participation in these schools which gives insight into the attitudes about education bearing upon the problem of community solidarity, but rather the characteristically Japanese manner in which they participated.

The relationship between the community and Miss Ada Mahon, the principal of the Bailey Gatzert School, illustrates this point well. In the twenty-five years or more since she took over the supervision of the Main Street School, and later of the Bailey Gatzert School, Miss Mahon has come to symbolize leadership in the educational work of the community, and because she assumed full responsibility for this leadership, the community tended to give her cooperation in anything she proposed. Not alone for her intellectual influence but even more for her moral influence, has she been appreciated by the community, and it is undoubtedly the moral goals which she emphasized in her school that have made her thoroughly acceptable to the community. The community attitude has been, then, to accept the leadership of Miss Mahon for a large part of the educational work of the community, and they have turned over full responsibility for this work, on the grammar school level, to her.

Because of this responsibility taken over by her and her school, the community feels a certain obligation to her. It is interesting to note the way in which they have attempted to repay this debt. In 1920, when plans were being laid for a new school building in the community to replace the old Main Street School, the community offered to raise the sum of $10,000 to aid in its construction. When the offer was refused by school officials on the ground that the building was to be a public one, the community donated an expensive moving-picture projector instead.[58] A few years ago, as an expression of their gratitude to Miss Mahon for the work that she had done, the community raised a sizeable sum of money with which they sent her on a tour of Japan, and the large reception held in her honor at the time of leaving left no doubt as to the obligation felt by the community towards her. Likewise, in the Washington School district, adjacent to that of the

---

[57] Ninety-five per cent of the pupils of Bailey Gatzert School in the center of the Japanese district are Japanese. Central, Pacific, and Washington have large minorities of Japanese pupils.

[58] Katherine Lenz, *Japanese-American Relations in Seattle* (unpublished master's thesis, University of Washington, p. 16).

Bailey Gatzert, the parents of that area gave Mr. Sears, the principal there, a gift of a trip to Japan.

On the grammar school level it seems that the parents, while they defined their own task as that of reinforcing the teacher's instructions, placed the responsibility of instruction directly upon the teachers themselves. This inclination was enhanced by the unfamiliarity of the Japanese parents with the American mode of instruction, which necessitated their relatively complete dependence upon the schools themselves for their children's training. There was nevertheless the obviously fundamental trust which the Japanese place upon formal education, and the apparent lack of recourse to pragmatic methods of instruction. The parents conceived their chief task to be that of reinforcing the authority of the school, and of repaying obligations to the instructors.

It was quite recently that the main interest in education shifted more definitely to the high school level, for only in the past five years or so has the peak of Japanese high school population been reached. (See Figure IV.) Most of the Japanese students in Seattle entered one of the three high schools in the vicinity of their community—Broadway, Garfield, or Franklin. In recent years about one-third of the Broadway School students have been Japanese, and in a lesser degree a like aggregation of Japanese students has concentrated at Garfield and Franklin. Despite this fairly high concentration of Japanese students, however, their parents have carried on little active association with the schools, undoubtedly because of the presence of a greater white student body. Therefore, instead of controlling their children by cooperation with the teachers as was frequently the case on the grammar school level, in the high school there was a more direct passing of responsibility on to the children themselves.

Perhaps the basic pattern for industry in school was already laid in the grammar schools. In any case, zeal for scholastic effort was not lacking as is shown by the numerous honors which Japanese students have won out of all proportion to their numbers in school.[59] It is true that extra-curricular honors, too, were sought and frequently won by these students, but seldom were they won at the expense of lower scholarship standing. In fact, there seems to be some correlation between the excellence in grades and participation in extra-curricular activities, which raises questions as to the possible incentives to industry which the families of such students might have given.

Of course, not all parents ambitiously seek scholastic excellence for their children, but, unquestionably, a large majority emphasizes scholastic achievements.

---

[59] A record of valedictorianships and salutatorianships awarded to Japanese students in the nine Seattle high schools between the years 1930 and 1937 is as follows:

	Valedictorians	Salutatorians
1930	1	0
1931	0	0
1932	0	1
1933	0	1
1934	1	1
1935	3	0
1936	1	1
1937	3	2

Some evidence of this point is found in Mrs. Katharine Woolston's study of standards of living among the Japanese in Seattle, in which she shows that the Japanese spend a far greater proportion of their income for "advancement" than the average Seattle family, and a relatively closer proportion to the ideal standards determined by experts.[60] It is because of their concern for their children's advancement, that they bring pressure to bear upon their children for a more arduous pursuit of their studies. Some of their commonest admonitions are: "The second generation come of a great heritage and they must prove their greatness." "The first generation immigrants had to sacrifice much to give their children the kind of education they are getting, and the second generation must show their gratitude by making the most of it." "In Japan the students study hard because entrance competitions are so keen, but the American students have it too easy." There is, in the Japanese family, a competitive drive towards supremacy, and the above-mentioned admonitions are frequently used by the parents to make their sons and daughters study harder.

It is not family pressure alone that has stimulated scholastic efforts of the students, but a constant community reinforcement of the position taken by the families has been an added incentive. For example, in earlier years it was customary for the Seattle Japanese Association to present, at the time of graduation from high school or university, an especially large leather-bound notebook to the students graduating with honors, and a smaller notebook to those graduating without such honors. In later years, with the increased number of graduating students, it became impossible for the Association to continue such gift-giving, but today they still gather at dinners for the graduates, and there is always special recognition awarded those graduating with honors. In newspapers, in churches, and in street conversations, there is always a tendency to single out the students with outstanding scholarship. In this way the community brings pressure to bear upon the students in a most significant manner. With widespread recognition and emphasis of this kind being awarded to high scholarship, the competitive tendency inevitably grows among the students to a remarkable degree.

These ideals of education, which are sufficient explanation in themselves to the parents for the unusual scholastic success of their children, also function to support community solidarity. Some of the common rationalizations made among the first-generation Japanese are based on the belief in a superior national background.

> It is very likely that parents of other nationalities do not think of their children as much as the Japanese do. It is a particular trait of the Japanese that they take a deep interest in the welfare of their children. No other national group in America, not even the Americans themselves for that matter, seem concerned about the circumstances and the future of their children as are the Japanese.[61]
>
> The basic reasons for the ability among Japanese young people to do well in school is that they have the will to win, and also the constant reminder from their parents that they must keep the family name at the front. The Japanese children

---

[60] Mrs. Katharine Woolston, *Japanese Standard of Living in Seattle* (unpublished master's thesis, University of Washington, p. 29).

[61] Document SX5.

are trained, under the constant urging of their parents, to think that they must become great, and in consequence they work hard at their studies. It's probably true that they don't develop their social side as much as the Americans but they're too busy for that.[62]

Following the announcement of several Japanese valedictorians and salutatorians in the Northwest in 1937, a local Japanese newspaper editor wrote in his columns:

> That they [the second generation] are, in general, by heredity, of a superior quality, we must recognize.
> This is equivalent to saying the Japanese people are of a superior biological quality; but the way in which they have surpassed the white students in all fields of high schools and university, and shown their superiority, almost makes them out to be of an entirely different class.[63]

By these successful forays into the scholastic field, at least from the standpoint of the measurable honors which their children have won, the Japanese parents find means of reinforcing their group sentiments. As the last quotation from the newspaper article points out, these scholastic differences place the Japanese, at least from their own point of view, in an entirely different class. It reinforces the belief, which otherwise would be extremely uncertain, that the Japanese can by sheer power of their superior qualities overcome any adverse circumstances standing in their way, and thus relieves them of the need to seek aid from the whites. It further emphasizes the efficacy of the "we-group" and the necessity for continuing to work as a community in promoting this kind of success.

Today at the local University, one may see the effect of this emphasis upon educational superiority in the increasing number of Japanese students enrolling for higher education, primarily with the hope of improving their economic status. In the matter of sending their children to college, opinion is divided. Some place very strong emphasis upon it, others recognize its necessity for boys but not for girls, while still others, observing the self-made men of the community, stress the greater necessity for a practical training. But the weight of opinion tends to be on the side of giving the children as much education as possible, and thus the enrollment increases at a rapid rate.

In this whole movement, however, one important question has not been raised; the question as to exactly where all of this is supposed to be leading. In the same news article quoted above, the editor declares: "We do not question the fact that in the end the persons of outstanding excellence will win out."[64] But what is the measure of outstanding excellence? The Japanese believe the grade rankings given to the Japanese students in high schools an accurate measure of their racial excellence, but are not these grades a measure merely of a certain type of ability? Are these superior scholastic standings truly a measure of a capacity for life adjustment, which is after all the final criterion of worth, or does this particular type of application tend, at the same time, to limit the horizon of the student's world view?

---

[62] Document SX8.
[63] *The North American Times,* June 15, 1937.
[64] *Ibid.,* June 15, 1937.

It would seem to one evaluating the facts from an unpartisan point of view, that the whole emphasis upon scholastic success as a measure of superior personal quality reflects a typically Japanese characteristic in thinking about life in general. What the first-generation Japanese have done in training their children for application to their studies is without doubt highly commendable, and they can perhaps be justly proud that their sons and daughters have won the scholastic laurels that they have. However, their failure to broaden the children's outlook upon life by opening other vistas of knowledge than those found in textbooks, and their failure to emphasize more the pragmatic test of living, the ability to reflect upon new situations as they occur, shows the tendency of the Japanese to view society as a relatively static structure. Undoubtedly, this is a heritage from the recent feudal background, but the Japanese have not raised the question as to whether the formalized feudal frame of reference is suitable to a mobile industrial society.

Yet, not alone with the public schools and universities do the parents stop in their efforts to pour formal education into their children, for when the American schools are dismissed, the children are sent daily in the late afternoon to attend the Japanese Language School. When the school was first started there was some opposition on the ground that it was unnecessary. One person relates:

> At the time when we first started the school, there were many in the community who fought against the idea, and declared that there was no necessity for such schools since their children were to be American citizens.... The Japanese consul, at the time, also felt there was no need for the teaching of the Japanese language to these young people.[65]

But today there is general agreement that ability to speak the language is an absolute necessity for the second generation, not only to provide wider social intercourse with the older generation, but because their economic relationships are in large part with the first generation, or with some branch office of a Japanese corporation, and a knowledge of the language becomes almost essential in getting a job. Many American-born Japanese see their economic future in Japan, or in trading with Japan, and this again is an incentive for getting a good grasp of the language.

Today there are 1,250 students enrolled, thirty less than last year, and there is certainty of further decrease in future enrollment because of fewer numbers in that age group. In spite of all the efforts made to teach the second generation the Japanese language, the school has given only the merest foundation of fluency to a major portion of its pupils. What the school has done more successfully is to inculcate in its pupils through the reading of their text-books certain moral ideas that are typically Japanese. It has also served to solidify the community by requiring common participation in the institution. For, lacking as they do any governmental revenue for financing and administering the school, it has been supported by the people of the community, who have offered their services and their money to keep the school in operation. The Japanese, continuing strongly in their faith that the school is indispensable to the community, have given much of their time and money to its support.

---

[65] Document SX17.

In the promotion of education within the Japanese community, therefore, solidarity is furthered by the constant application of Japanese values to the educational institutions, and by the enforcement of these values upon the second generation. In the first place, the attitude of the community is one of idealizing formal education and, in consequence, there is relatively little experimentation on the part of the children with ideas that might tend to break down the community solidarity or develop a desire to break away from the community. These attitudes apply inherently in the case of the first generation since they had been bred in that tradition, but we see in the case of the second-generation group an extension downwards of the same ideas and points of view. In the second place, this tradition, with its emphasis upon scholastic competition among the Japanese, and its interest in gaining recognition, within the community, turns the community inwards. Moreover, when they look out upon the larger white community, because of the scholastic distinction of the Japanese students, a further emphasis upon the differences between the two communities is made. Lastly, in their stress upon the necessity for a training in the Japanese language, we have a multiplicity of factors supporting community solidarity.

Socio-Political Institutions

The Japanese Consulate. If all the Japanese living in Seattle were to be ranked according to position in the community, there is no question as to who would stand first. The Japanese consul, as a symbolic substitute for the nation and the Emperor whom he represents, has a pre-eminence unmatched by any, regardless of wealth or of personality among the Japanese in Seattle. The people render him the accord which the Japanese have long been trained to give any representative of the Emperor, and this recognition of authority follows clearly defined patterns of respect and obligation.

Yet, in spite of the regard the people have for the consulate, it must be recognized that in essence the consular office and the community are dissociated. While it is true that the consulate can bring strong controls to bear upon the community, in actual practice the consul is never so rash as to impinge too much upon the community's activities. Thus, when an important event or celebration that is distinctly a part of community life takes place, the consul is generally invited in an honorary capacity, but he seldom has any direct administrative control over the event. It is only where the community function is clearly related to the nation of Japan that the consular office assumes actual control, as, for instance, when some notable visitor from Japan comes to the city of Seattle.

The importance of the consulate, however, has not always been the same. Between 1901, when the office was first established, until the passing of the Immigration Act of 1924, the relationship of the consulate to the community was primarily that of a visa office for the Japanese migrants. Since 1924, however, the function of the consulate has shifted increasingly from the duty of overseer of the migrants to defender of the Japanese immigrant settler's position. For the Japanese immigrants, lacking the right of franchise as they do, the strength of the Japanese consular office has in no small measure compensated for their lack of citizenship.

Fundamentally, therefore, the value of the consulate to the community has increased in proportion to the increase in strength and status of Japan as a world power. Here, too, is an explanation of the Japanese tendency for all faces to turn towards Japan, for where they lack strength as individuals, they find in the power of a nation the courage to voice their own cause and defend their rights. In the community agreement concerning their orientation lies the strength of their community solidarity, for having as their focus of attention the same authority, the whole group tends to be controlled by the same motives.

With the increase in power of Japan there is created a necessity among the people to defend the cause of that nation more vigorously, for with each rise in national status new problems arise out of the growing complexity of international relations. Thus, during the recent Sino-Japanese wars, the community has felt it obligatory to cooperate extensively with the consulate in propagandizing the Japanese cause. This obligation is born of the fact that the first generation, for all their long years in America, still cannot forget the training of loyalty to their nation which they learned years before. Moreover they feel deep in their hearts that if the Japanese nation were not so powerful as it is, the immigrants in America would be trodden under foot by the Western peoples.

The consulate functions to solidify the community not so much by its authoritarianism or leadership, but rather by the participation which it demands of the people in certain types of activity that serve to reawaken in them memories of their native land.

The Japanese Association of North America. Where the Japanese consulate is necessarily a control from outside the community, the Japanese Association is in all respects at the focal center of the community. In fact, the consulate itself recognizes the superior position of the Association as the central control agency of the community, and the former carries on the major portion of its business with the community through the latter office. Yet to think of the Japanese Association as being the central agency in terms of final authority is misleading, for on the whole its function is far less that of leadership than that of a central coordinating agency.

One finds that the Association functions more in the capacity of managing those activities which have the sanction or the authorization of the community at large, and the net effect of their varied activities is a reinforcement of the attitudes which are behind the community. On the one hand the organization has come to fulfull those requirements that in Japan would be carried on by the government, and on the other hand it has taken over those tasks that in their native town life would have been served through a more stable family system than exists here, or through an informal body of the community folk. The organization is, therefore, in many ways a peculiar combination of bureaucratic activity, so familiar in Japan, and the informality of a small village group that meets to consider some highly localized problems. It is probably because the Association fits into these patterns so familiar to the people of Japan that it contributes to the solidarity of the community, but, on the other hand, it is probably for the same reason that the organization is not as satisfactory as it might be in finding solutions for problems created in a new environment.

As with the other organizations which we have discussed, the functions of the Japanese Association have shifted with the changing tides of the times. Between the first organization of the Association in 1900 until the passage of the Immigration Act in 1924, the principal tasks of the Association were those dealing with immigration and the immigrants. There were the problems of visaing the passports, there were the problems of Americanization, and out of these developed also the questions of naturalization and anti-Japanese agitations.

In the earliest days it was customary for the consulate to act as the visaing agency, but this office, it was discovered, was not close enough to the people to render this service satisfactorily, and the work was turned over to the Japanese Association. Thus, from a very early period distinction of function between the Japanese consulate and the Japanese Association was made, and the naturally closer position of the Association to the people was recognized. The fact is significant in pointing to the peculiar fitness which the Association had for coordinating certain necessary functions of the community, and it is in this sense that the organization has contributed most to the solidarity of the community.

For a people who possess a natural respect for authoritarianism, and for government, it is not surprising that they considered the problems of Americanization, from a very early period, as being an important part of their program. Their efforts were directed mainly in the channels of American cultural education for the adult Japanese. More important still were their services in translating and interpreting important items of English news, both current and historical.

The natural consequences of such programs as those sponsored by the organization was an arousal of interest in naturalization and in gaining the rights of citizenship. Thus, when one of their members, K. Ozawa, brought his case before the Supreme Court in an effort to win the right of franchise, the Association fell directly behind the movement, and organized a committee to press the suit. That the Japanese Association was in those days showing leadership cannot be denied, and the importance of its work has come to be minimized largely because of its failure at that time to overcome the prevailing anti-Japanese feeling.

Perhaps the outstanding efforts of the Japanese Association came in the years immediately following the enforcement of the Anti-Alien Land Laws. Though these laws affected more immediately the peoples of the rural districts, they nevertheless had important bearing upon the Japanese in the city because they were aimed at the Japanese people as a whole. Here again the Association took the initiative in bringing the cases to court, but failing in these law suits, sought other means of getting around the problem. It successfully met the situation by the formation of a corporation under the trusteeship of some white lawyers, and under its name bought up some eight hundred acres of land which it redistributed among the Japanese farmers who had lost possession of their land.[66]

On some occasions, therefore the Japanese Association has served in the capacity of community leadership, but essentially because of its failure to defend successfully the cause of the Japanese in these important cases, the organization has never attained the dominant position in the community that it might have. Its impotence as a vigorous political group within the community, which it was necessary that it become were it to serve the community significantly, lay in the fact that not one of its members had a right of franchise under the laws of the United States.

Feeling keenly this lack of strength in their own hands, the leaders of the Japanese Association worked to gain this power indirectly through their children, who, being born on this soil, could have that which the elder Japanese could never possess. We find, therefore, that it was the Japanese Association which was instrumental in creating the Japanese-American Citizen's League, a body of second-generation American citizens. But even since the creation of the League, there has not been any marked increase in strength of the Association, and, as a matter of fact, it is playing a less important role today than before because of the decreased significance of its work.

Yet, on a small scale they continue the activities which I earlier indicated as being reinforcements of sanctioned attitudes within the community. In brief, the program of the organization is divided into five departments, namely, Finance, Social Welfare, Commercial, Educational, and Young People's Welfare. To finance the organization, the people of the community contribute annually in the way of dues and donations a sum of $3,186.50, supplemented by a donation of almost $1,000 from the Emperor of Japan, plus about $3,647.99 which it receives from the Community Chest. With regard to the last item, however, the community prides itself on the fact that it returns more in the amount it donates at the time of the Community Chest drive than it receives from the Community Chest, and it likes to see its name in the American newspapers described as among the first communities to go over the top in the drive.[67]

The Social Welfare Department has as its chief activities the work of caring for the dependents of the community, aiding them in whatever manner necessary, returning to Japan those who desire to go back there but have no financial means of getting there, visiting hospitals where Japanese are present, and caring for the cemeteries where Japanese are buried in any numbr. In its expenditures for the year 1936, the accounts of the Association show an expended sum of $1,623.25 for relief and visiting. It has an annual banquet honoring those more than seventy years of age, and a meeting honoring the mothers because "Japanese women have relatively few occasions when they can get out and enjoy social contacts."

[66] Document SX17.
[67] Treasurer's Report, The Japanese Association of North America, 1936-1937.

The Commercial Department works in conjunction with the Japanese Chamber of Commerce promoting the Japanese business men's cause. For instance, on the Fourth of July it puts on a celebration in the Japanese community for the purpose of attracting white customers to the Japanese business district. It acts as arbiter between the numerous business associations that go to make up the Chamber of Commerce.

In its educational program, its chief aim has been that of promoting high scholarship among the second generation, and it has been among the most vigorous supporters of those students who have taken special honors at their schools. Likewise is it the watch-dog for any cases of juvenile delinquency, that they might be publicized as a moral lesson to other children. It is this kind of pressure which keeps the parents constantly watchful over their children, lest they fall into bad ways and bring shame upon the family name.

Lastly, it supports a Young People's Welfare Department, the purpose of which is to promote interest among the young people in the Association's work. One member of the organization gives the reason for this program as follows:

> It is certain that the Japanese, as long as they exist as a racial unity, must function as such. No matter how much they may desire to become Americans, as long as their color is different, it will be impossible for them to withdraw completely their bonds from the Japanese community. This problem of racial difference is perhaps the most important one which the Japanese must meet.[68]

In this brief history and outline of the Japanese Association we can see that while the organization has not functioned significantly in the way of creative leadership in the community, it nevertheless has had an important part in binding the community together. It is to be noted in the program which we have just briefly described that its main framework is underlaid with conceptions that are essentially Japanese in tradition. Financing of the organization, for instance, is by donations, gifts, and dues paid as an obligation that must be met by the community. Its commercial programs, its educational work, social welfare and young people's welfare are all directed towards an increased consciousness of that which is peculiarly Japanese about its community and which necessitates an increased participation within the Japanese community.

When we view some of the attitudes held by the people of the community concerning the Japanese Association, we recognize that the solidarity which it supports is not as secure as would at first seem. When we look at the members of the organization, we find that a great number of them are like this individual who declared:

> When I first came to this country, I didn't join any special organizations. The only thing that I did join was the *Nihonjinkai* (Japanese Association) but that was because everybody else in the store was a member and they urged me to become one also. It only meant that I paid my dues, but I never went to any of the meetings. The only advantage gained by it was that I was known to be helping in a public cause.[69]

---

[68] Document SX5.
[69] Document SX20.

And there are still others like the following who feel that the Japanese Association is of interest primarily to those who are particularly eager to gain recognition from the community, and feel quite critical about the organization:

> What good is the Japanese Association anyway? I used to pay one dollar a month to them, but I tell you that an organization like that can't do any work on a little bit of money. . . . All that those fellows do down there is to get together and talk about each other. They never do anything useful for the community.[70]

> The Japanese likes being recognized as some super-individual. The Japanese Association is composed entirely of men who are after recognition, and who would be the leaders themselves if they could get into the place of power. Some of the older men still hold the seats of honor, but there are a number of younger men who are struggling to get up there themselves. I think this desire for recognition is especially a Japanese characteristic and one sees it in the activity of almost every associational group among the Japanese. . . . It's also true of the Japanese women as well.[71]

It would seem from this that the future of the organization depends upon the course of history, and any critical events that may occur during that historical process. If the community continues in its present uneventful course, the Japanese Association may soon find itself without any business by which to retain the interest of the people. If some crisis should arise as, for example, a vigorous anti-Japanese campaign, then the Association may again come to life and show not only a coordinating value, but real leadership as well. Judging by present indications, though we can see that the community has sufficient Japanese orientation as yet to offer certain functions for the Association, it would seem that the Japanese Association of Seattle will gradually pass into senility in the not distant future.

Kenjinkai. I have already mentioned the important part which the *ken,* or the prefectures of Japan, have played in creating the solidarity of the Japanese community. We need here to mention something about the formal organization behind the *ken,* that is, the *kenjinkai* (prefectural organization).

In Japan, the *ken* as a social organization has relatively little importance, except as an administrative unit of the nation. It is only when the Japanese leave their native land and congregate in large numbers in alien places that the differences of *ken* become noticeable and make for a degree of intimacy among those of the same *ken* that has a certain clannishness about it. The chief reasons for this felt difference is, of course, the fact that over long centuries of relatively immobile social organization, the people living in different areas developed distinctive traits of culture which differ so greatly from one another that even from the standpoint of language alone there are occasions of great difficulty in understanding. Even today, with the high degree of mobilization and standard education that have entered into Japan, there continue some of these differences.

Miss Fumiko Fukuoka puts the point well where she says:

> The Japanese who comes to America, a strange land, is exceedingly happy to meet any other Japanese, and more so when they are from the same *ken.* They feel an intimacy which they did not know when they were in their home land. They feel

---

[70] Document SX11.
[71] Document SX7.

as if they have known each other a long time and are kinsmen. In the early days of Japanese immigration, the number of *kenjin* was small. In later years the newly arriving immigrants found a considerable number of *ken* people in America. They got together and organized friendly clubs.[72]

Here in Seattle it cannot be so boldly stated that a considerable number of *ken* people came together, for with the relatively smaller community here than in Los Angeles, about which Miss Fukuoka is writing, the size of the *kenjinkais* has necessarily been smaller. It is for this reason that the local *kenjinkais* have not attained to the high degree of organization that they have in some places in California.

Yet the functions of the *kenjinkai* have been the same here as elsewhere, though perhaps on a smaller scale. Informally speaking, the organization is simply a social gathering of people from the same prefecture having, therefore, a common background of memories, speech, and customs that offer the members of the group an intimacy which they cannot feel with people from other *ken*. Formally speaking, the clubs function in the much more significant capacity of mutual aid, giving help to those members who are financially embarrassed by illness, death, or a lack of economic means. The financing of the organizations is largely carried on by donations, but due to their somewhat obligatory character among Japanese, these donations take on the characteristics of dues.

It is perhaps more in the informal functions of the *kenjinkai* that we see their most characteristic solidifying effects. *Kenjin*, for example, are said to differ in their personality traits depending upon the *ken* from which they came. Common belief is that the Hiroshima people are sharp business men, the Gumma people are quiet, and so on. Throughout all these comparisons is a constant tendency to elevate one's own group. Parents desire their children to marry someone from their own *ken*, because, they say, it is then easier to trace the heredity of the other party. One always has a tendency to have more friends among one's own *kenjin*, and there is a tendency to favor a *kenjin* in any kind of relationship. Not the least important are such *kenjinkai* social functions as their annual picnics, their frequent dinner meetings for one occasion or another, and their sponsorship of gatherings for any distinguished person of a *ken* passing through the city.

At one time, large blocks of *kenjinkai* people participated in the Japanese Association, and it was possible for the larger *ken*, such as the Hiroshima and Yamaguchi, to gain considerable control over the Association and its important offices. Because of the disfavor with which these blocs were held, particularly by the people of the smaller *ken*, the political significance of the *ken* has since declined considerably, but even today there is a tendency to give a greater prestige to those having membership in a large *ken*.

The *kenjinkai*, it may be said, is an extension of kinship attitudes to the group next larger than the family and closest to it in the degree of intimacy among the members. We may conceive it as standing midway in the scale of relative intimacy from the family to the community. In this sense it shows a broadening of the bonds of mutual obligations to include a larger primary group than

---

[72] Fumiko Fukuoka, *op. cit.,* p. 16.

one's immediate family. It is in this last function of acting as a relay in the passage of primary-group attitudes from the family to the community that organizations like the *kenjinkai* contribute significantly to the solidarity of the community.

The Japanese Newspapers.   There are today in the Japanese community two Japanese daily newspapers, excluding the weekly paper published by a second-generation Japanese. The function of these two newspapers in creating solidarity in the community lies not so much in any leadership which they show with regards to community activities as in their function as agencies of publicity for the other organizations of the community, and in particular for the two main socio-political bodies, the Japanese consulate and the Japanese Association. It is primarily in the work of publicizing such organizations, and in thus keeping the eyes of the community turned inward, that the newspaper is a significant factor in strengthening solidarity.

While this writer was unable to find any readily accessible figures on the circulation of the newspapers in the city of Seattle, it is probable that most first-generation Japanese have access to either one or the other of them, since there are not many of these immigrants who read the American papers. Because only a minimum of first-generation Japanese read the American newspapers the Japanese newspapers are significant, for here, then, is an important organ for the formation of public opinion which has an almost uncontested supremacy.

Although traditionally the two newspapers have shown a keen rivalry in attempting to gain the widest support of the community and have frequently taken opposite sides of issues in support of their differences, at bottom there is little distinction between the two except petty differences of policies which they have fashioned for purposes of publicity, for they are both weighted heavily in the direction of a Japanese orientation. Today, however, one of the newspapers has a wider and more popular support, not only here in Seattle alone, but throughout the Northwest, and, according to the word of a person familiar with the financial conditions of both, it seems inevitable that one of the two must sooner or later be discontinued.[73]

No better illustration of the kind of influence which the Japanese newspapers have in making for the solidarity of the community is to be had than in the type of news which these two papers have published over the recent Sino-Japanese conflict. Since the beginning of warfare in July, 1937, the papers have covered with unabated avidity all the important news to be had about the Oriental crisis, and there has not been a day since that time when the war news was not the most important item on the front page. Not alone in the fact that they give so much space to this event do we have the significance of this news in furthering the solidarity of the people, but rather in their consistent and vigorous defense of the Japanese cause in this war do we see the peculiar influence which it has. That their news is weighted heavily in that direction is not surprising when we consider that all their news items from Japan are direct transcripts of daily wireless

[73] Document SX16.

dispatches taken through their own receiving stations directly from Japan, and when we note that this news is censored by the Japanese government before it leaves the nation.

The powerful effect of this publicity is apparent in the solid attitude of the community in support of the program to which the Japanese government has committed itself in China, and the vigorous and bitter attacks that the people make against the American newspapers which, they claim, deliberately falsify their reports in favor of China. In this regard, it is interesting to note that the Japanese newspapers, in conjunction with the Japanese consulate, have sponsored a program of educating the second-generation Japanese concerning the "true" conditions behind this conflict, as a counterbalance against the evil influences of the American dailies published here in Seattle. Thus, in their news and editorial columns, one finds admonitions to parents to interpret the Japanese newspapers to their English-speaking sons and daughters so that the latter may correctly state the case to the larger American public.

The following are typical of the attitudes expressed among the Japanese parents today concerning the inadequacy of interest taken by the second-generation in Japan's cause in this present conflict:

> The trouble with the second-generation is that they read only the *Times* and the *P. I.,* and they can't get anything but lies about the whole situation. The Japanese newspapers say that it's not so much the matter of educating the American public with the Japanese point of view which is necessary, but it's more necessary to make the second generation themselves understand what the whole thing is about for they can't read the Japanese newspapers and they don't sympathize with the Japanese angle of it for that reason.[74]

> In these times it is too bad that the second generation cannot read the Japanese papers. It is really a tremendous handicap. The second generation ought to have a clear conception of what is taking place in the Far East, but without this ability to read the news they are not in a position to serve as an interpreter to the Americans of the Japanese position. Even now, the Association is looking for some capable Japanese student from Japan, or some *kibei,* who can serve in this capacity.[75]

The function of the Japanese press in this community is clearly that of articulating those sentiments in the community which are latent and oriented towards Japan, particularly in crises such as the present. There have been occasions when these papers have assumed for themselves the function of Americanizing their public, but by the very nature of the papers, written as they are entirely in Japanese, except in relatively recent years when it became necessary to give over one of their daily eight pages to an English section to attract the growing second-generation population, the newspapers have a natural bent towards directing the public's mind toward Japanese interests.

Not alone with regard to such news as that of the recent conflict is the press important in orienting its readers toward the community, but in so far as it gives over a major portion of its paper to discussing matters which are largely Japanese, from the editorial down to the novelette, the influence of the press in keeping the people turned toward the community is extremely profound. Here too

[74] Document SX7.
[75] Document SX11.

are daily reported the organizational activities of the community, and all the births, marriages, deaths, and other events which go to make up the body of the community's daily conversation. Not the least important is the use which the Japanese Association or the Japanese consulate makes of these columns to guide the Japanese community in channels which they desire. For instance, one of the chief means of juvenile delinquency control used by the Association is that of publicizing in the newspapers the immoralities of any youngsters whom they learn about, and this undoubtedly exercises a strong influence over the parents of the children if not directly over the children themselves.

The solidarity of the community is promoted by the newspapers, primarily, by the emphasis which they give to news which is essentially of Japanese or of their community interest; secondly, by the necessarily Japanese interpretation which they give to any general news; thirdly, through the efforts made by organizations to control the community through its columns; and finally, because its readers need not learn to read the American newspapers.

RECREATIONAL INSTITUTIONS

Play for the average Japanese in Seattle has not been a significant part of his life. After all, the Japanese have had to struggle long and hard for the little they have earned, and there has been relatively little time or money left over for recreation. But in the recreational activities that they have developed, we can plainly see the same forces making for solidarity in the community that have been at work in the other institutions.

If we observe the play of the younger generation, we find no difference whatsoever in their round of recreational life from that led by normal American youths. They play at all the sports from baseball to ping-pong, they know how to dance, they get together _for_ nightly poker sessions, but the play of the young people is, in general, not at all similar to the play of the older generation. It is true that a limited number of the latter have taken to tennis, golf, and even to skiing, but by and large the first generation knows nothing at all about these games, or they tend to remain merely observers.

Among the first generation there is an inevitable tendency to turn to those forms of play that fit essentially into a Japanese world of things. They play not the international form of chess, but a Japanese brand. In music, they know nothing of the Western flute or guitar, but they have their own Japanese flutes and guitars ("shakuhachi" and "biwa") that make music strangely unmelodious to the Western ear. And if it be true that fishing is one of the most popular of sports among the Japanese, it is essentially because the Japanese are traditionally fish-eaters and have a far greater appreciation of a good catch than have the Americans.

The significance of the fact that their play does revolve about values that are essentially Japanese in their background is that for the participants in these activities there is a constant reinforcement of the orientation towards Japan, and even a reference back to their childhood days in their native land. One of the best examples of such reinforcement lies in the Japanese entertainments that are frequently presented at their local auditorium. In the main these plays, such as the "kabuki," are mostly in the heroic tone, and the parts are played with primary emphasis upon the traditional ideals of the Japanese people such as filial piety, the courage of warriors, and the acceptance of duty. The plots revolve, as a rule, about problems of duty, and they are filled with the traditional sentimentalism of Japan which is as much a part of Japanese culture as the burlesque is a part of American culture. Through such entertainment the Japanese are able to transport themselves back to another life and another land. One who knows the sentimental attachment which the Japanese feel for their home land can realize how effectively these repeated dramatizations draw them back into their community.

Again, in the enthusiasm which the first generation show for such traditionally Japanese sports as *judo* (art of self-defense) and *ken-jutsu* (Japanese fencing) do we find expressed values that are typically Japanese by nature. Not only are these physical exercise, but as an English dictionary defines correctly, a mental development as well; for a primary function of these sports is a disciplining of the will. The recent enthusiasm shown among the second-generation Japanese in these sports is undoubtedly in large part a reflection of the enthusiasm shown by their parents, for the latter see in these sports a means of giving their sons a form of discipline which they feel is lacking in America.

Finally, we may turn to the reading matter of the Japanese. Few among them read even the American newspapers, and to find any of them reading an American book would be so unusual as to create amazement. But, in their native language, they are relatively extensive readers and there are but few homes where there are not a few Japanese magazines available or where there is not a book-shelf of Japanese books. That they read, on the average, anything more profound than the sort of thing to be found in a popular American magazine is dubious, though books on religion seem to have an exceptional interest for the Japanese readers. But, as in the case of the past few months when books on the Sino-Japanese war crisis have been particularly popular, the effect of their reading is to strengthen the Japanese points of view, and revive their Japanese interests.

Play among the Japanese of Seattle, therefore, serves to reinforce sentiments toward Japan, for the whole of their play life tends to revolve about activities that are essentially Japanese in character. Where they do participate in games that are American in tradition, it is invariably among themselves, and there is but a limited assimilation into the spirit of the culture out of which the game springs.

IV.

CONCLUSION

The problem of social solidarity which we have discussed in the foregoing chapters is an old one which has occupied the attention of some of the most eminent sociologists. Maine, Tönnies, Durkheim, Cooley, and Thomas, to mention but a few outstanding names, gave considerable space to its discussion. While it might be desirable to offer in this connection an extended analysis of these men's writings on this subject, it is impossible to enter upon such a digression at this point. There are, however, certain points of agreement in their writings on social solidarity that should be mentioned.

They all observe, for instance, that in societies where social solidarity is strong the people implictly assume a kinship basis for the group; or when this kinship is not real, the people take it to be real. This implies that the solidarity of such societies grows out of their primary-group intimacy and the bonds of collective responsibility which such kinsfolk intimacy establishes. These writers also point to the dominance of tradition in the collectivistic societies, and the levelling out of personal differences which such conformance brings about. By contrast the individualistic societies are seen to have a minimum of tradition, a greater degree of rational or deliberative activity, and, hence, a greater individuation of personality.

Among the Japanese in Seattle the fundamental factors that have contributed to the solidarity of the community are undeniably of this very nature. It is not difficult to see that one of the central tendencies of the community is constantly to refer for social guidance to certain customary modes of behavior which were imported from Japan. The fundamental character of these customs, we have pointed out, is their invariable tendency to call out sentiments of collective responsibility. We thus find that the central authority in the Japanese community which keeps its people disciplined and solidary lies in the weight of tradition, and that this authority is sustained by the people's continued belief that these customs are righteous and fundamental.

We do not, of course, take any such naive position as that traditions live in and of themselves apart from the men who make and use them, but traditions have a peculiar authority for the Japanese because social life has little meaning except in reference to them. It is not possible for the Japanese to make their world as they go along, as the Western individualists, relatively speaking, do. The Japanese live, rather, in expectation that their world will be patterned after the traditional Japanese mode of behavior, and they find themselves at loss when these expectations are not met. The judgments of the past constitute the authority which compels the Japanese to create a highly integrated community, and they have no alternative, for these people have no knowledge of other ways.

More specifically, this body of tradition commands permanence and worship because it has as its cornerstone a code of ethics that has received the sanction of the ages. The historicity of this code of ethics gives it an aura of sacredness for the Japanese, and when this code is applied as the backbone of their traditions so as to make the rejection of this tradition unethical, the people have no other choice than to conform.

But if men are too long exposed to a system of ethics that is inconsistent with their personality, they may come to lose faith in it, and find serious need for questioning it. In the Japanese community, it is essentially this lack of any necessity for questioning their ethics that makes for the persistence of it. When, from the smallest social unit to the largest there tends to be a rigidly consistent application of the same ethical code, a participant in such a community cannot help but feel an inner rationality in his traditions.

If, however, traditions of the American community, such as individualism, were to make inroads into the Japanese community, the greatest amount of social pressure from the defenders of Japanese traditions could not prevent the disorganization of their ethics. It is in this regard that the orientation of the Japanese in Seattle is important. From the first the orientation of a large majority of the people has been directed towards Japan; because of this orientation they built a community that is socially self-sufficient, and in this way prevented the invasion of any alien culture. The anti-Japanese agitations and legislation further acted to drive them into their own community. The net effect is that the community, though scattered geographically for business and residential reasons, is in spirit a tightly bound enclosed circle through which their traditional modes of ethical behavior operate without interruption.

Under such circumstances has grown that spirit of *Gemeinschaft* which Tönnies so clearly described. No more succinct statement as to the relationships of men among the Japanese could have been made than when he said: "One finds himself in a community with his own people from birth onward, bound to them in weal and woe." This is precisely the way a Japanese feels when in his own community—that he is with his own people, and that the welfare of the one is the welfare of the many. It is through this that his faith in his ethics is doubly strengthened.

But to think that there is continuous solidarity is, indeed, erroneous, for one may logically expect that in a society of this type there would be factors tending to disrupt the smoothness of its operation. If, as our analysis would seem to indicate, such a society places high valuation upon status, and by the movement from Japan to America the possibility of attaining high status is increased, we may expect among the people a vigorous striving towards the elevation of the self within that group. So we find in the Japanese community a constant struggle for social supremacy that creates much bickering and petty competition. One finds today a few in the community who have tired of this oppressive intimacy, and have chosen to break away to a large degree.

Aside from such factors as personal ambitions, however, there seem to be other seeds of disruption of which the Japanese themselves are not so clearly aware. Especially is this the case where, by the necessity of participation in an American social order, the Japanese community finds at points here and there that their primary-group conceptions of society are inadequate to meet the demands of a new type of social participation. In other words, try as the Japanese may to keep the invasions of individualism and other secondary-group attitudes from seeping into their community, by the very nature of their contacts with American institutional life they have begun to find certain conflicts, between their mode of life and that of the American, that cannot be reconciled except by completely casting off the one or the other. Since they live in an American scene, it seems necessary to cast off their Japanese customs rather than the American ones.

Here, too, is one way of explaining assimilation among a people accustomed to a ghetto life in America. We see in the breakdown of solidarity, as a consequence of dilemmas created within their own community, the steps by which the Japanese are led out of their community. It is where their traditional mode of behavior is no longer consistent with the actual life they lead, where the traditional obligations become burdensome and the personality cries for liberation, and where attitudes of sacredness about the traditional Japanese customs degenerate, that assimilation into another group starts to take place in earnest.

Finally, we may conclude our discussion by raising the question as to what significance this study has in understanding the solidarity of communities other than that of the Japanese. To generalize from a single case is, of course, unsound, but it may be permitted to state a hypothesis which might be tested by others.

In the Japanese community we have found that the basis of solidarity lies fundamentally in tradition, a tradition that is closely interwoven, in the main, with time-tried conceptions of ethics. The question to be raised is whether there exists any relation between the ethics and the social solidarity of other communities.

Our emphasis upon the ethical as the chief factor in community solidarity, we recognize, comes from the fact of having studied a people among whom ethics seems to have an outstanding importance. Yet even a casual knowledge of the United States, with its extreme segmentalism of cultural organization and an underlying lack of any clearly defined ethical tradition, makes one wonder if lack of solidarity and lack of ethical agreement are not closely correlated. Is it not possibly true that those people among whom the sense of "oughtness" is least clearly integrated are those among whom the lack of solidarity is most apparent?

It is not my suggestion that the United States should adopt the ethical tradition of Japan, for even now we observe that these feudal values are beginning to show inconsistencies within themselves under the pressure of industrialism. Rather is it my point that the apparent lack of integration within the communities of America is, perhaps, a product in part of a lack of well defined ethical meanings, and that some more mobile set of ethical traditions than that of the Japanese might be developed to give American society a greater stability. Sociology may function here in raising such questions as: What conception of ethical meanings exists among the American people? What are the inherent inconsistencies within their ethical tradition? What kind of ethical conception may be defined that will give greater integration to their culture, and will be acceptable to the people? In other words, I contend that sociology may, perhaps, study with profit the ethical aspects of a society as well as the statistical, for the one is as much a set of sociological data as is a collection of statistical tables.

BIBLIOGRAPHY OF WORKS CITED

Ayusawa, Iwao Frederick, *Industrial Conditions and Labor Legislation in Japan.* Geneva: International Labor Office, 1926.

Buell, Raymond Leslie, *Japanese Immigration.* Boston, World Peace Foundation, 1924.

Burke, Kenneth, *Attitudes Toward History,* 2 vols. New York: The New Republic Company, 1937.

————, *Permanence and Change.* New York: The New Republic Company, 1935.

Carpenter, Niles, "A Study of Acculturalization in the Polish Group of Buffalo, *Monographs in Sociology,* No. 3, Buffalo: Buffalo University Press, 1929.

Cooley, Charles Horton, *Social Organization.* New York: Charles Scribner's Sons, 1929.

De Becker, Joseph E., *Annotated Civil Code of Japan,* first edition. London: Butterworth and Co., 1909.

DeBenneville, James Seguin, *More Japonico,* published by author. Yokohama, Japan: "Gazette Press," 1908.

Durkheim, Emile, *The Division of Labor in Society,* translated by George Simpson. New York: The MacMillan Co., 1923.

Fukuoka, Fumiko, *Mutual Life and Aid Among the Japanese in Southern California With Special Reference to Los Angeles.* Unpublished master's thesis, University of Southern California, 1937.

Galitzi, Christine A., *A Study of Assimilation Among the Roumanians in the United States.* New York: Columbia University Press, 1929.

Gulick, Sidney L., *The American Japanese Problem.* New York: Charles Scribner's Sons, 1914.

————, *Evolution of the Japanese,* fourth edition revised. New York: H. Revell Fleming Co., 1905.

Hayner, Norman, "Delinquency Areas in the Puget Sound Region," *American Journal of Sociology,* XXXIX (November 1933) 314-328.

Hearn, Lafcadio, *Japan, An Attempt at Interpretation.* New York, London: The MacMillan Co., 1904.

Hibino, Yutaka, *Nippon Shindo Ron,* translated by A. P. McKenzie. Cambridge, Great Britain: Cambridge University Press, 1928.

Hiller, E. T. and Corner, Faye, "A Study of the Descendants of an East Frisian Group," *University of Illinois Studies in the Social Sciences.* Urbana, Illinois: University of Illinois Press, 1928.

Ichihashi, Yamato, *Japanese Immigration, Its Status.* San Francisco: The Japanese Association of North America, 1913.

————, *Japanese in the United States.* Stanford University, California: Stanford University Press, 1932.

Inouye, Jukichi, *Home Life in Tokyo,* second edition. Tokyo: The Tokyo Printing Press, 1911.

Iyenaga, Toyokichi and Sato, Kenoske, *Japan and the California Problem.* New York: G. P. Putnam's Sons, 1921.

Japanese Immigration; An Exposition of Its Real Status, a report prepared by the Japanese Association of the Pacific Northwest, 1907.

Japanese Census of Seattle: 1925, 1930, 1935, Reports Prepared by the Japanese Association of North America in Seattle.

LaViolette, Forrest, *Types of Adjustment of American-Born Japanese.* Unpublished doctor's thesis, University of Chicago, 1938.

Lentz, Katherine Jane, *Japanese-American Relations in Seattle.* Unpublished master's thesis, University of Washington, 1924.

Maine, Sir Henry J. S., *Ancient Law,* new edition. London: J. Murray, 1930.

McKenzie, Roderick D., *Oriental Exclusion.* Chicago: The University of Chicago Press, 1928.

Mead, Margaret, *Cooperation and Competition Among Primitive People.* New York: McGraw-Hill Book Co., 1937.

Mears, Eliot Grinnell, *Resident Orientals on the American Pacific Coast.* New York: American Group, Institute of Pacific Relations, 1927.

Millis, Harry Alvin, *The Japanese Problem in the United States.* New York: The MacMillan Co., 1925.

Nishinoiri, John Isao, *Japanese Farms in Washington.* Unpublished master's thesis, University of Washington, 1926.

Nitobe, Inazo, *Bushido, the Soul of Japan,* seventeenth edition. Tokyo: Teibei Publishing Co., 1911.

North American Times Year Book, 1936. Seattle, Washington: North American Times Daily News, 1936. Also for 1911, 1916, 1928.

Ogura, Kosei, *A Sociological Study of the Buddhist Churches in North America With a Case Study of Gardena, California, Congregation.* Unpublished master's thesis, University of Southern California, 1932.

Park, Robert E., *The Immigrant Press and Its Control.* New York: Harper and Bros., 1922.

Park, Robert E., Burgess, Ernest W., and McKenzie, Roderick D. *The City,* Chicago: The Chicago University Press, 1935.

Park, Robert E. and Miller, Herbert A., *Old World Traits Transplanted.* New York and London: Harper and Bros., 1921.

Rademaker, John A., "Japanese in America," *Our Racial and National Minorities,* Edited by Brown, Francis J. and Roucek, Joseph S. New York: Prentice-Hall Inc., 1937.

———, *An Ecological Study of the Japanese and Chinese in Seattle: 1912 and 1932.* An unpublished manuscript.

Redfield, Robert and Villa, Alfonso, *Chan Kom, A Maya Village.* Washington, D. C.: Carnegie Institute of Washington, 1924.

Redfield, Robert, "Folkways and City Ways," *Renascent Mexico,* Herring, Hubert and Weinstock, Herbert. New York: Covici Friede Publishers, 1935, pp. 30-48.

Sansom, G. B., *Japan, A Short Cultural History.* New York: The Century Company, 1931.

Smith, William C., *Americans in Process.* Ann Arbor, Michigan: Edward Brothers Inc., 1937.

Stein, Gunther, "Made in Japan," *The Forum Magazine,* XCIV (November 1935), pp. 290-294.

Steiner, Jesse Frederick, *The Japanese Invasion.* Chicago: A. C. McClurg and Company, 1917.

Taft, Donald R., *Two Portuguese Communities in New England.* New York: Longman's, Green and Company, 1923.

Takeuchi, Kojiro, editor, *Nippon Immin-Shi.* Seattle: North American Daily News, 1928.

Thomas, William I. and Znaniecki, Florian. *The Polish Peasant in Europe and America.* New York: Alfred A. Knopf Inc., 1927.

Tönnies, Ferdinand, *Gemeinschaft und Gesellschaft.* Berlin: K. Curtius, 1922.

U. S. Bureau of the Census, *Fifteenth Census of the United States: 1930 Population,* Vol. II. Washington: Government Printing Office, 1933.

Wirth, Louis, *The Ghetto.* Chicago: The University of Chicago Press, 1928.

Woolston, Mrs. Katharine, *Japanese Standard of Living in Seattle.* Unpublished master's thesis, University of Washington, 1926.